A VIEW FROM A WINDOW

A VIEW FROM

A WINDOW

Heather Angel

Salem
House

Salem House Publishers
Topsfield, Massachusetts

To Martin, who shares my new-found enthusiasm
for gardens.

First published in the United States by Salem House Publishers,
1988, 462 Boston Street, Topsfield, MA 01983.

Library of Congress Cataloging in Publication Data
Angel, Heather
    A view from the window.

    Includes index.
    1. Gardens—Pictorial works. I. Title.
SB465.A54   1988   712'.6   87–12996
ISBN 0–88162–241–9

Designed by Norman Reynolds
Typeset by Latimer Trend & Company Ltd, Plymouth
Printed in Italy by New Interlitho SPA

CONTENTS

FOREWORD

ALTHOUGH I trained as a zoologist and worked as a marine biologist, my interest in, and love of, plants goes back to my childhood. Long summer holidays were spent on my grandparents' Suffolk farm where my grandmother taught me the names of wild flowers. As a nature photographer I have sought wild plants in bogs, in deserts, in forests, in rivers and up mountains, all over the world. My interest in gardens developed later. It quickened when working on my book *A Camera in the Garden*, as I came across plants I had photographed in the wild in different continents, sharing the same bed in British gardens.

The origins for this book began during my second visit to China in 1985 when I led a small photographic delegation from Britain. It was April when I visited the restored gardens in Suzhou for the first time. The azaleas were in full bloom and I was fascinated by the ornamental windows, especially in the Cang Lang Ting (Green Wave Pavilion) where several days' work would be needed to make a complete photographic record in different lights of more than a hundred lattice windows. A book on Chinese windows was too specialist to be commercially viable, but gradually the idea of a book on gardens viewed from windows emerged.

Since I travel a good deal abroad in the course of my work as a photographer, I started to make detours specifically to look at gardens. I began researching views from windows in British gardens early in 1986, initially drawing up a tentative list of the gardens already known to me. The list was extended by scanning garden books for photographs which showed the house or other buildings overlooking the garden. Surprisingly, in my researches I found that remarkably few books on garden design list windows in the index. It soon became apparent that, despite the expressed concern of some garden designers for the view looking out, the results in most cases provide a rich setting for views on to the

house—an extroverted, rather than an introverted attitude to the relationship between house and garden. However, a careful search in many a garden revealed features such as apertures in walls and hedges opening on to views, whether expansive or secret, which previous writers had not considered worth a mention. To discover the 59 views featured in this book, I had to visit three times that number of gardens, so had to resist finalizing the selection for as long as possible. Although my aim was to include a wide variety of garden styles, the final choice reflects my preference for formal designs, as well as a fascination for China and a love of Gertrude Jekyll gardens. The 1987 summer was late, cold and sunless; indeed, June was the wettest on record— keeping to a tight schedule was a nightmare. Hawk-eyed readers will notice my most productive day was on 18 June, when I managed to photograph three gardens. Until I had visited a garden and knew the viewpoint, I could not begin to write about the view.

Without exception, everyone whom I approached for access to their garden, or for suggestions of possible sites, was most enthusiastic about the project. For selection, not only had a view to be sufficiently photogenic to warrant a full page reproduction, but also it had to illustrate a noteworthy aspect of garden design. Inevitably this meant that many interesting gardens had to be omitted because they were not framed or overlooked by convenient windows; while some intriguing windows had no garden vista worth recording. For example, the moon gate in the red wooden Chinese bridge at Grey's Court in Oxfordshire looks out on to a field in one direction and on to branches of a copper beech with a distant view of the house in the other. The views from the windows in the historic tree house, with the gothick interior, at Pitchford Hall in Staffordshire unfortunately are now obscured by the gnarled branches of the ancient lime tree in which it rests. Gardens are by nature transitory. A change of ownership may lead to delapidation, while the progressive trend towards a reduction in the number of gardeners results in labour-intensive parts of the garden being redesigned. However, unexpected discoveries such as the descending series of circular apertures at Castle Tor (p54) and the ice window in Harbin (p118), were additional bonuses.

The apertures used to photograph gardens featured in this book vary from conventional windows in houses, to openings in hedges, gates, walls, garden buildings and even, ice sculptures. The gardens vary greatly in size, age, topography, elevation, aspect and, not least, in the man hours needed to maintain them. Some are frequently open to the public, others only occasionally, some not at all. So that the average gardener can relate to them more easily, medium or small-sized gardens have tended to be selected in preference to well-known grand vistas from stately homes. It is hoped that many of the private gardens, in particular, will stimulate ideas for readers to modify and incorporate into their own particular terrain and climate. Because every garden is unique, any attempt to replicate a successful garden design can never work. Ideas for colour combinations or plant associations can, however, be gleaned and modified to suit. Few of us have the foresight to visualize the final effect of a mature garden and throughout garden books, references can be found to planting associations achieved by 'happy accident'.

The choice of gardens included in this book is obviously a personal one and, no doubt given time, other photogenic window views would have come to light. There are some obvious omissions; notably the splendid view from the tower at Sissinghurst on to the white garden, where increasing pressure from visitors has resulted in a decision by The National Trust not to permit any professional photography in the garden.

In every garden there is a continuous process of development and decay on different time scales. For example, annuals bloom and fade in a matter of weeks, while robust woody plants can continue growing through many decades and trees for several centuries. Here in Britain, although we are able to grow a very wide variety of plants, less hardy plants tend to be crowded out by vigorous neighbours or else succumb completely in adverse weather. Even if a garden is constantly maintained, it continues to evolve from one year to the next. An accurately dated and clearly defined photograph therefore provides an invaluable reference point in the history of a garden. Throughout this book there are references to early photographs assisting in the restoration of neglected gardens; hence the date when each photograph was taken has been included in the caption.

A natural disaster on the scale of the hurricane which hit south east England in the early hours of 16 October 1987, wrought havoc to trees in gardens and parks, as well as in hedgerows and woodlands. The picture of Kew Gardens taken from the top of the pagoda is therefore already historic, for five hundred trees were lost and a further five hundred were damaged in this garden alone.

Although in later years Gertrude Jekyll suffered increasingly from myopia, she developed an amazing ability to critically observe everything around her. If nothing else, I hope this book will encourage an increased perception of windows in relation to house and garden; maybe even their consideration as a feature in garden design.

This may have been one of the most time-consuming books on which I have ever worked; it has also been one of the most enjoyable.

Heather Angel

Farnham, October 1987

7

INTRODUCTION

NATURAL views through windows can be found in rocks and rotten trees. Caves were the earliest form of shelter utilized by man, for protection both from the elements and wild animals. Each day, he arose to a familiar view through the simple window on the outside world—a view which changed with the seasons. Man's passion for imitating natural features in eighteenth century English gardens, led to the construction of grottoes simulating dark caves with bright apertures lit by natural light at Stourhead in Wiltshire, or by artificial light in the subterranean grotto at Goldney (p130).

The origins of the word window date back to the old Norse word *vindauga* meaning 'wind-eye' from which the Middle English word *windowe* was derived. We tend to take windows for granted today. During the day we frequently glance out of windows, yet how often do we take a second look at the shape of the window or the structure of the window frame? The original function of windows was to let light and fresh air into dwellings and unwanted smells to drift out. They also needed to be an effective barrier against bad weather or to filter harsh sunlight in low latitudes.

Windows play a vital part in creating a favourable microclimate inside the home. In cold climates, they need to be well insulated to prevent heat loss to the outside; hence the introduction of double glazing (or even triple glazing as seen in Harbin, China's ice city). On the other hand, windows in dwellings in tropical climates need to be constructed so as to reduce heat and glare in the house. In the Middle East desert region, the intense heat from the sun is reduced by a projecting cornice over the lattice window which cuts down glare as well as filtering cool air into the house. Lattice windows are also used in Egypt to help reduce glare; known as *mashrabiya*, they are made from many small turned wooden pegs arranged to make attractive silhouetted patterns when viewed from within against the

Natural rock window in Stone Forest, Yunnan, China. 5 March 1986

bright light outside. Hot air can be cooled and desert dust filtered, by hanging palm frond mats, moistened by regular soaking in water, over the windows.

Open apertures provide the clearest view from a window. Before glass was invented, mica, horn, marble, oiled linen and rice paper were used as substitutes. These, like early glass were translucent rather than transparent, filtering out some of the light as well as providing hazy images of the view beyond. In recent times, central eskimos used either a translucent sheet made from seal gut or a block of clear ice as a window in their *iglu* made from snow blocks. The translucent window shells, produced by a particular oyster in the Pacific Ocean, now so popularly used to make lamp-shades in the west, also function as a glass substitute in the Philippines.

Natural glass, formed by rapid volcanic eruptions, was used by prehistoric man for his arrowheads long before the first man-made glass was created in Egypt, around 4000 BC, as a substitute for semi-precious stones. From here the techniques of glass manufacture spread throughout the Mediterranean. Although glass was used in windows in Roman Britain it was seldom less than an eighth of an inch thick and coloured so that the daylight passing through had a green or greenish-blue cast. During the fifth and sixth centuries the design of domestic buildings regressed; the windows became simple apertures for letting smoke out and wooden shutters were used to exclude wind and rain. Glass making became a lost art. In AD 675 Bishop Benedict Bixop of Wearmouth in County Durham, brought French workers over to glaze the windows of his church and cloisters. However, the use of glass did not extend to domestic buildings at that time.

In Saxon times, windows made a building vulnerable to attack, so they tended to be narrow slits set high in thick walls. Oiled linen and parchment were used as a substitute for glass, but it is not known how they were fastened to the windows. Thin ground panes of horn were held in place by channelled lead strips in a similar way to the glass panes in leaded lights. Norman windows tended to be long and narrow and were typically round-headed.

As law and order was gradually established, manor houses no longer needed to be fortified. Glass became more widely available, and as the size of windows increased, they tended to become much more ornate. In the second half of the thirteenth century, the introduction of glazed windows by Queen Eleanor of Provence (wife of Henry III) and her daughter-in-law Queen Eleanor of Castile (wife of Edward I) meant English castles were no longer riddled with draughts. At this time, windows in domestic buildings were either rectangular or had pointed heads. Where two or more lights were placed within a semicircular or pointed arch, the area above the window arches was filled in with carvings; later on, this was pierced with circular, trefoil or quartrefoil openings, known as *plate tracery*.

Although the window size increased in Britain, single sheets of glass could not be made large enough to fill the window and so the leaded window was devised. Small panes of glass, known as *quarrels* were held in place by lead strips called *cames*. The leaded glass panes were stiffened by wooden or stone stays—the vertical ones known as *mullions*, the horizontals as *transoms*. In the fourteenth century, true window tracery developed with curved bars of stone supported on mullions. In addition to this development of the window, more peaceful times led to gardens gradually replacing moats.

Even by the end of the fifteenth century, glass was still expensive and, since labour was relatively cheap, the Earl of Northumberland used to have the window glass taken out of Alnwick Castle, in Northumberland when he was not residing there, as a precaution against its being

Haddon Hall Gardens glimpsed through clear glass pane in Long Gallery. 3 July 1987

blown in by the wind during severe weather.

A particularly fine example of late sixteenth-century mullioned windows can be seen at Hardwick Hall in Derbyshire. Indeed, they dominate the west front of the house designed by Robert Smythson and built for Bess of Hardwick, the Countess of Shrewsbury, in 1591-7. The windows increase in depth with each successive floor, for all the principal state rooms, including the High Great Chamber, are on the upper floor. From the window on the landing outside the Chamber there is a grand overview of the Main Garden. The formal knots and parterres laid out by Lady Louisa Egerton Gordon in the nineteenth century have now gone, but the four compartments formed by a yew alley and a hornbeam alley crossing it at right angles, remain.

An unusual undulating mould was used to make the leads for the diamond glass panes of the windows in the upper floor of the Long Gallery at Haddon Hall, also late in the sixteenth century. When the windows are viewed from outside, some portions appear dark and some appear light, depending on whether light is passing through or being reflected from the panes (p67). This is clearly shown in William Robinson's engraving of Haddon Hall in his book *The English Flower Garden*. The mould was found at the turn of the century and has been used during the restoration. Each piece of diamond-shaped glass is set at a different angle from the adjacent panes to create a decorative effect. A similar design can be seen in the Elizabethan manor house of Snitherton Hall, also in Derbyshire, which may have been copied from Haddon. This detail of a window at Haddon Hall illustrates how the curved windows, and the imperfect sixteenth-century glass with copious air bubbles (highlighted by the shadows cast on the sill) contribute to a distorted view of the garden. The past practice of etching names and poems on the panes using diamond rings, further detracts from seeing any detail

beyond. A single pane of more recent, unblemished glass provides a clear image of the rose blooms outside.

After the imposition of window tax in 1696, several windows in larger houses were stopped up so as to avoid the taxation. Since this tax was levied on the number of windows, regardless of their size, it resulted in both a reduction in the number of windows and an increase in their size—they became taller. In 1766 houses with seven windows or more were taxed and in 1798 this was extended to include houses of six windows. Until the repeal of the window tax in 1851, new houses were built with recessed areas where windows could be inserted at a later date.

Towards the end of the seventeenth century, the quality of window glass was much improved, so the view from a window became less distorted. When duty was imposed on glass during the reign of William and Mary, it was found to be counter-productive and was soon halved and finally repealed after three years. In 1745, excise duties were introduced on all imported glass as well as being levied on the raw materials used for the manufacture of glass in the United Kingdom. Before the glass tax was repealed in 1845 the method of assessing the duties changed many times. The abolition of glass tax and of window tax at a later date, allowed window glass to become more widely used in all kinds of houses.

Until architects began to draw up designs for houses, builders created them according to local tradition. This meant regional styles were perpetuated until building manuals were printed and distributed nationwide. Then distinct national styles developed and one of the ways of dating a building is by studying the window design. Early in the seventeenth century, the side-hinged casement window allowed ventilation control. By the end of the century, when the quality of glass improved, the sliding sash window began to replace the casement windows. During the Regency period (1810-20) when

Brick mosaic maze based on the Tudor rose at Kentwell Hall. 13 October 1987

ironwork became fashionable, windows were adorned with metal canopies and wrought iron balconies. During the Victorian era, windows were often decorated with ornate surrounds.

The production of new materials such as steel, aluminium and concrete during the present century opened up a new approach to the construction of buildings and windows. Large areas of sheet glass allowed huge picture windows to give views uninterrupted with horizontal or vertical bars; although nowadays economic factors and climate both govern the size and number of windows in a house.

Over the centuries man has sought to improve on nature, by creating attractive views not only from his own house, but also from garden buildings or through walls, by judicious positioning of plants or architectural features. In Tudor Britain, raised walks or mounts provided elevated views from which to appreciate the garden layout or views beyond. A particularly fine example was made in 1533–4 in the Mount Garden at Hampton Court, with a three-storey-high glass arbour on top. The windows in this arbour looked down on to the Privy Garden as well as the adjacent river Thames.

Knot gardens, a popular feature of the sixteenth-century pleasure garden, were designed to be viewed from above so they were typically sited in Privy Gardens where they could be overlooked by the sovereign. Elizabeth I and her entourage tended to spend the summer months touring country estates, where knots were created, often at short notice, beneath the windows of her apartments.

The design, and hence the solution, of a maze (particularly a hedge maze) is also best appreciated from an elevated viewpoint. Many hedge mazes, together with other formal features, were destroyed by the sweeping landscape views required by 'Capability' Brown, but the yew hedge maze planted at Hampton Court in 1690 remains today because Brown had orders not to touch it. Mazes are becoming fashionable once again, and several have been laid out in recent years. A highly original and particularly striking brick maze, was laid out in the courtyard of the Elizabethan manor house of Kentwell Hall in Suffolk in 1985. Based on the Tudor Rose, the brick paved mosaic maze is, like Tudor knot gardens, designed to be viewed from the upper floor windows overlooking the courtyard. Although constructed in only two dimensions, the paths are laid out in such a way that they pass over or under one another, thereby creating a three-dimensional puzzle.

China, above all countries, uses the window as a device to link one part of the garden with another by luring the eye beyond a solid wall. The division of the garden into smaller units makes it appear much larger than in reality. Windows of every shape abound in classical Chinese gardens. The extent of the view seen through an open aperture depends on the size, the proximity of the nearest object and the extent of decorations within the frame. Most simply, a small unglazed Chinese window frames a single plant (p118); while a larger aperture frames a vista with pavilions, walkways, water, rocks and plants. The seventeenth-century writer, Li Li-Weng, conceived the idea of having a permanent frame to the changing scenery as he rowed across West Lake in Hangzhou, simply by cutting fan-shaped windows in the sides of his boat.

Windows in Chinese gardens may be infilled with intricate geometric shapes (p124) or naturalistic scenes of birds and flowers (p126). These kinds of windows are features in themselves; partially obstructing the view to the other side, they provide tantalizing glimpses of foliage or a coloured wall beyond. An unusual decorative window can be seen in the Humble Administrator's Garden (Zhuo Zheng Yuan), the largest of Suzhou's old gardens, originally laid out in the Ming Dynasty (AD 1368–1644). Within the Thirty-six Mandarin Ducks Hall a magnificent blue glass window frames the Bamboo Hut Pavilion across the water. As the sun shines through the window, blue shapes are projected on to the grey stone floor.

When the Chinese-American architect Ieoh Ming Pei was commissioned in 1978 to design a hotel in the scenic area outside Beijing known as Fragrant Hills Park (Xiangshan), he used designs based on traditional architecture behind walls in the gardens of Suzhou, Wuxi, Hangzhou and Yangzhou. He chose white for the exterior walls, since this provides the maximum tonal contrast for silhouettes of adjacent bamboos or pines, whether projected by sunlight or moonlight. Inside the main reception area of the Fragrant Hill Hotel a large moon gate frames vertical rocks in a pool, while rows of diamond-shaped apertures look down from corridors in upper floors and large quatrefoil windows frame plants inside or views on to the garden.

The mid-eleventh-century houses of Japanese noblemen formed a complex series of buildings. In front of some compartments, gardens were created in small open courts or *tsubo*. Here, wisterias, flowering cherries or plums were grown in tubs and the name of the dominant flower would often be given to the lady whose room overlooked the small court.

Over many centuries the delights of viewing gardens from windows have been extolled and decreed by various writers. John Harvey in *Mediaeval Gardens*, records how Bishop Guillaume de Passavant built a stone manorhouse at Le Mans in 1145–58 and a garden '. . . for those leaning out of the hall windows to admire the beauty of the trees, and others in the garden looking at the fair show of windows, could both delight in what they saw.' André Mollet in his *Jardin de Plaisir* (1651) laid down the concept of the unified French formal garden as a design to be appreciated from the main windows in the house. 'To the rear of the house, the *parterres de broderie* must first be set out, so that they can be seen and enjoyed from the windows, without any obstacle in the form of

Blue glass window in Humble Administrator's Garden, Suzhou, China.   3 May 1985

Quatrefoil windows in Fragrant Hill Hotel near Beijing. 9 February 1987

trees, fences, or other high objects which might interrupt the view.' Beyond would be turf parterres, statues on pedestals, and various water features, notably fountains and canals. Among the French formal gardens created at this time on a lavish scale was Vaux-le-Vicomte designed by André le Nôtre, laid out in 1657–61 and restored at the end of the nineteenth century. Like Versailles, also designed by Le Nôtre, the main axis was designed to be seen from the house.

Philip Miller wrote in his 1731 *Gardener's Dictionary*: 'In a fine Garden, the first thing that should present itself to the sight, is a parterre, which should be next to the House, whether in the front or on the sides, as well upon account of the Opening it affords the House, as for the Beauty with which it constantly entertains the sight from all the windows on that side of the House.' David Stuart in *Georgian Gardens* argues that by the 1790s the garden was being designed to be seen from within the house, and so contributing to the pleasure of the occupants.

Humphry Repton clearly appreciated the importance of the view from within by repeated references to views from windows. Remarking on Barningham, Norfolk in *Fragments* he writes: 'There is no subject connected with landscape gardening of more importance, or less attended to, than the window through which the landscape is seen.' Again in his Red Book for Honing Hall, Norfolk he writes: 'I always distinguish by the name of Park that portion of wood and lawn which is seen from the windows of a mansion. With respect to its size there is one variable rule, viz. it must appear to have no boundary.'

Long before photography was invented, Humphry Repton used pictures to communicate ideas to his clients. When he began practicing as a professional landscape designer in the eighteenth century, he believed this was an art which could be perfected only 'by combining the skills of the landscape painter and the practical gardener'. Had he been alive today, he might well have substituted 'photographer' for 'landscape painter'. In his Red Books he painted watercolours, often with movable flaps, to present 'before' and 'after' versions of a vista. In this way Repton was able to show his client a visual interpretation of the end result—something photography can do only with the use of models or artwork overlays.

The revolution in window design during this century, has made both architects and landscape designers aware of the importance of the window in relation to garden design. The architect, Edwin Lutyens, was always mindful that the garden's appearance from the house was equally as important as the way the house appeared from the garden. When he and Gertrude Jekyll worked together on a joint project, they would discuss the relationship between the house and garden. Richard Neutra, the German architect, often incorporated the view from the window as an integral part of the houses he designed in America. In the 1950s Perkins House at Pasadena in California, the pool outside the living room extends into the room itself by passing beneath a full height plate-glass wall. The transparent effect is so convincing, it is difficult from inside the house to determine the exact line separating the interior from the exterior.

Russell Page in his book *The Education of a Gardener*, stresses the importance of the view from a window in small properties: 'An average small house is likely to have an average small garden and this fact immediately suggests that we must shape and style the garden as it will be seen from the house. The importance of the house in its garden setting as seen from outside will be of secondary importance.' The international designer, David Hicks, believes: 'Apertures are extremely important in any garden design. A tall, narrow gap between hedges, an opening in a wall, the way through from one part of a garden to another lends excitement and drama to the atmosphere of the garden.'

John Patrick, in his book *The Australian Garden*, describes the trouble a couple took to plant their Canberra garden to be viewed from a large semicircular bay window. The major plantings were achieved by one person positioning each plant, directed by the other looking out through the window. Eventually, by constant reappraisal, the prime location for each plant was obtained.

By no means all windows successfully frame a garden view, since the pictures seen in the frame depends on many factors, not least the size of the aperture, the distance of the feature from the window and the aspect the window overlooks. Although small apertures, notably bull's eye and eyebrow windows, restrict the angle of view outside, they can make attractive features in themselves. For example, at Monticello, in Virginia, the home of Thomas Jefferson, there are six ornamental bull's eye windows in the drum of the third floor dome room. Four of these windows overlook the west front gardens with partial views of distant mountains. When small windows overlook a completely enclosed garden, such as a courtyard, the only way to photograph the entire area, is by opening the window and leaning out with a wide angle lens on the camera.

The views from modern picture windows, on the other hand, offer no subtle hint of what lies beyond; they are always blatant. If they overlook a road, they are a distinct disadvantage, for unless screened by net curtains, which obviates the purpose of having a large window, pedestrians get an excellent view into the house. Thomas Church, the American landscape architect, suggested using a living screen as an effective barrier if it can be distanced from the window so as not to block the view outside. Working with the warm Californian climate, Church successfully integrated modern houses with glass walls so the garden became an extension of the house. The extreme wide angle of view offered by picture windows makes it difficult to include

Courtyard of Hostal de los Reyes Catolicos at Santiago de Compostela. 29 March 1987

17

the entire vista in a photograph taken through them.

A room with windows facing different aspects provides a variety of views illuminated or cast into shadow with the passage of the sun throughout the day. In letters written c AD 100, Pliny the Younger, describes in detail the views from rooms in his Laurentian Villa on the west coast of Italy and he also explains how windows with different aspects gave access to the sun at various times of day. A small bedroom '. . . lets in the morning sunshine with one window and holds the last rays of the evening sun with the other . . . there is a room built round in an apse to let in the sun as it moves round and shines in each window in turn.'

An unusual functional window feature can be seen in the Jacobean boundary wall of Stanway House in Gloucestershire. Three pairs of oval peep-holes or spectacle windows were used by promenaders on the raised grass terrace inside the garden to view visitors approaching the gatehouse outside. Visitors were unable to see in, since there is a 10ft/3m drop from the bottom of the windows to the road outside.

Nobody with an aspect overlooking the coast, wants to blot it out, and on sites subjected to strong winds, a panel of safety glass can be inserted into a wall or fence as a windbreak allowing views of the garden (or coastal scenery) beyond. Similarly, houses facing the harbour in the Spanish port of Corunna, have glass-fronted balconies so they can enjoy the changing vista in any weather.

For accounts of gardens published before the invention of photography, we have to rely on written descriptions with or without sketches, scale drawings or artists' impressions. The disadvantage of the written word is that it may not mean exactly what it says. Even without any written account, evidence for the design of past gardens can be gleaned by examination of the garden scenes depicted in embroideries and through open windows as backgrounds to portraits. In the late fourteenth and early fifteenth centuries, Flemish artists in particular, such as Jan van Eyck (d 1441) have provided invaluable glimpses of the gardens during this period. In a painting of the Virgin and Child in a summerhouse by a follower of Hans Memling (c1490), the view outside the window shows rectangular beds laid out in a formal design with shrubs clipped in the form of *estrades* with circular well-spaced tiers. A later painting entitled *Arthur, first Baron Capel and his Family* by Cornelius Johnson c1639 (in the National Portrait Gallery, London) shows exquisite detail of a Stuart formal garden with terracing, balustrades, statues and fountains at Little Hadham in Hertfordshire.

As Thomasina Beck elaborates in her fascinating book *Embroidered Gardens*, past trends in garden design are also depicted in contemporary embroidered furnishings, notably on sixteenth-century cushions, table carpets and bed hangings. In many embroidered valences, details of 'carpenter's work'— wooden framework tunnels clothed in plants—are depicted showing numerous windows for looking out into the garden without being seen. Although it is impossible to identify individual plants from miniature garden scenes, contemporary flowers were often embroidered in detail on royal robes.

Throughout this book there are many accounts of how old photographs have aided in the restoration or reconstruction of derelict gardens. Whereas sketches or paintings may incorporate a certain amount of artist's licence, an accurately dated photograph may be the only way to confirm that a garden feature did or did not exist at a particular time. Photography is, therefore, an invaluable tool in garden design—providing the evidence is correctly exposed and sharply in focus.

VISTAS

FOR centuries, gardens in Britain had been enclosed; but by the end of the seventeenth century, influenced by the work of the French architect André le Nôtre who designed Vaux-le-Vicomte (1656–61) and Versailles (1661–1715), they began to expand outwards. Viewed from the first floor of the moated chateau at Vaux-le-Vicomte, the vista along the main axis runs from the *parterre de broderie*, past topiary shapes and pools with fountains, ending in a huge statue of Hercules. At both ends of Vaux-le-Vicomte, le Nôtre laid out vistas which radiated from a central point in the shape of a *patte d'oie* or goosefoot. He used this design repeatedly and with elaborations, as at Versailles, where the main axes were orientated along the compass points. From the windows of the Grande Galerie the vista is aligned with the setting sun.

Nearly all the British gardens modelled on the Versailles pattern have long since gone, but the giant *patte d'oie* of tree-lined avenues shown in Kip and Knyff's drawing (c1700) of Hampton Court still exists today. Along most of their length, the avenues are planted with limes, but adjacent to the palace the lines are extended into the semicircular area, shown as a parterre on the 1700 drawing, by a planting of conical yews. The central toe of the *patte d'oie* is formed by the canal known as Long Water.

Early in the eighteenth century, Charles Bridgeman played a leading role in the transition from formality to the open landscape gardens of William Kent and 'Capability' Brown. All three men participated in laying out the grounds at Stowe in Buckinghamshire. In Bridgeman's time, the plan included formal parterres around the house, with straight vistas and meandering walks beyond. A ha-ha was made at Stowe several decades after the first one was built in Britain at Levens Hall in Cumbria c1695. The ha-ha, a French innovation, is a dry ditch with a retaining wall which excludes stock from the garden, while still allowing a clear view of the countryside beyond the boundary. Vistas abound at Stowe; there are tree-lined avenues and open windows between clumps of trees giving views on to the countryside.

Bridgeman was essentially a garden architect, while Kent looked at garden design with a painter's eye. The best surviving example of Kent's landscaping is at Rousham in Oxfordshire. The garden was designed to be seen as a series of pictures which gradually unfold along the paths meandering past statues through open and wooded areas. From the house, the view across the rectangular bowling green (1720) looks past the Lion and Horse statue by P Scheemaker to fields and hedgerows in the Oxfordshire landscape. The lines of Kent's serpentine rill which flow through the cold bath, were to be repeated again and again on a much grander scale by Brown. At Blenheim Palace in Oxfordshire, Brown joined two lakes to make a large, sinuous stretch of water which passed beneath Vanburgh's bridge and he also created the lake at Petworth Park in Sussex by damming a stream.

None of the gardens featured in this section include vistas which define views framed by an avenue but, except for Kew (p22), they do show views beyond the garden boundary. In his *Education of a Gardener*, Russell Page advocates using a few trees or hedges near the house to frame the view and above all 'if there must be flowers they should be close against the house or below a terrace wall and so only visible when you turn your back to the view'. All the gardens featured here, with the exception of the valley garden at Glendurgan (p21) and the tiny walled garden set in a grassy field on Lindisfarne (p25), endorse this ideal, for they are essentially green landscapes.

A Cornish Glen

GLENDURGAN

There can be few sights to equal the view which unfolds before Glendurgan house near Falmouth in Cornwall. From early spring the garden is enlivened by a succession of colours as magnolias, camellias, rhododendrons and embothriums burst into bloom. The patches of colour harmoniously intermingle with exotic trees, set against a backcloth of native trees, all situated in a valley which plunges down to a cove, on a tidal part of the Helford River at Durgan village. On days when a sea mist creeps up the valley and this breathtaking view is obliterated, one feels almost cheated; but then the individual trees and shrubs which make up the spectacular landscape can be appreciated from closer viewpoints by making a complete circuit of the garden.

During the 1820s and 1830s, Alfred Fox, one of a well-known Cornish family firm of shipping agents based in Falmouth, laid out the garden and planted most of the large exotic trees, including two huge tulip trees *Liriodendron tulipifera*. He was able to ship plants from far flung locations to a corner of Britain where mild winters allowed many subtropical plants to flourish.

In 1833, Alfred Fox planted a cherry laurel *Prunus laurocerasus* maze—the only one of its kind in Britain today. It takes two men ten days to clip it with shears. The walk into the centre of the labyrinth and out again covers a distance of one and a quarter miles. The maze is planted on sloping ground and the best view of it can be seen from the opposite side of the valley.

Each successive Fox generation has made his own contribution to the garden. Alfred's fifth son, George Henry Fox, planted many conifers including cedars and cypresses as well as fragrant rhododendrons. After he died in 1931, his eldest surviving son, Cuthbert Lloyd Fox, introduced cornuses, camellias, magnolias, Asiatic rhododendrons and eucryphias which are now well established.

This view was taken in a year when spring came late to Cornwall after the severest winter in living memory. Fortunately this garden suffered few losses, although all the exposed fronds of the *Dicksonia antarctica* tree ferns died back completely. The valley sides below the house are left uncut until after a variety of wild flowers, including a profusion of bluebells, have flowered. Here, one of several century plants, *Agave americana*, a native of Mexico, can be seen. Depending on climate, these plants can take up to a hundred years before they produce a huge flowering spike, which fruits and then dies. An agave last flowered at Glendurgan in 1976. The Mexican drink *pulque* is derived from the fermented sap of the young flower head.

The two rhododendrons framing the view are 'Cornish red'. Behind the left one is a rare Formosan conifer—*Cunninghamia konishii* and a large *Thuja plicata*. To the right behind the flowering *Magnolia denudata* is a west Himalayan spruce *Picea smithiana*. Also in this view, near the centre of the picture are two Chusan palms, *Trachycarpus fortunei*. This palm was first introduced to Britain from China by Philipp von Siebold in 1830.

No visitor to Glendurgan can fail to be grateful that Mr and Mrs Cuthbert Fox and their son Philip gave it to The National Trust in 1962, so this notable garden, lovingly created and cared for by the Fox family for more than a century, can continue to be maintained for posterity.

The spring vista from the house down to the Helford river. 29 April 1987

A Grand Vista

ROYAL BOTANIC GARDENS, KEW

*V*isible from several miles away, the 163ft/50m high pagoda in the Royal Botanic Gardens at Kew, is one of several oriental follies designed by the architect Sir William Chambers when this part of Kew was laid out as a pleasure garden. Building began in the summer of 1761 and was completed in the spring of 1762. Horace Walpole, when writing to Lord Strafford on 5 July 1761, remarked, 'We begin to perceive the tower of Kew from Montpelier Row (Twickenham); in a fortnight you will see it in Yorkshire.'

Octagonal in shape, the pagoda rises nine storeys above the ground floor. The diameter of the first floor is 26ft/7.9m and the height 18ft/5.5m. Successively higher storeys have both the diameter and the height reduced by 1ft/0.3m. The pagoda is a shadow of its original glory, when glittering dragons, eighty in all, hung from the angles on the projecting roofs of each storey.

The Pagoda Vista was one of the many avenues and vistas designed by William Andrews Nesfield when he landscaped Kew during the 1840s. This spectacular avenue runs some 2300ft/700m from the rose garden adjacent to the Palm House to the pagoda. Over forty different kinds of trees were planted in opposite pairs but some have died and had to be replaced. This picture, looking north-east from a window at the top of the pagoda, shows the reverse view of the tree-lined Pagoda Vista to the right; the Temperate House is on the left.

Designed by Decimus Burton, the Temperate House was built over a period of almost four decades from 1860–1899 as, and when, money was available. It was originally planted with palms, tree ferns, camellias, acacias and subtropical crop plants—guava, mango and papaya from other glasshouses. Many large Himalayan rhododendrons were brought up from Cornish gardens for the North Wing (completed 1899) and as collectors returned with new Sino-Himalayan discoveries, these plants were housed in this wing until their hardiness was assessed. The yellow tree paeony *Paeonia lutea* from Yunnan was one of many plants introduced from China at the beginning of this century, causing great excitement when it bloomed in the Temperate House in 1900. The heating system gradually became more inefficient, and the house suffered bomb blast and weather damage, so it was completely restored during 1977–1980. As the original drawings were not available, a detailed survey had to be made of this scheduled building before work could commence. The light transmission has been greatly improved (before it sometimes fell as low as 28 per cent of the incident light) by using a redesigned narrow glazing bar made of aluminium alloy. The catchment and storage of rain water has also been increased. Throughout the reconstruction, the largest plants remained on site protected from the cold by polythene wraps and gas heaters. Within the Temperate House is a variety of half-hardy warm-temperate plants, arranged as originally intended, in geographical regions.

Chambers could not have envisaged the way his pagoda would have been used during the Second World War. Floor boards were cut away so that scientists could observe the way bomb models fell from a height. Well over two centuries after it was built, the pagoda at Kew remains one of Europe's architectural garden wonders, still making a superb focal point at the end of the Pagoda Vista, especially when it looms out of early morning mist.

The Temperate House and Pagoda Vista from the top of the pagoda. 19 May 1986

Defying the Elements

LINDISFARNE CASTLE

The relative inaccessibility of islands tends to make them an irresistible magnet, and the Holy Island of Lindisfarne off the Northumberland coast is no exception. At low tide, when a causeway links it to the mainland, visitors are lured across to Lindisfarne Castle. Rising from Beblowe Crag, the highest point of the island, the castle dates from 1549, when it was a fort. By the nineteenth century it had begun to decay, but in 1901 Edward Hudson was captivated by the site. He later bought the castle and commissioned the architect, Sir Edwin Lutyens, to create a country house for him. Hudson had intended to enlarge a pond in the field between the castle and a small walled garden, into a water garden; but the cost of restoring the castle escalated to such a point he had to discard this concept.

Lutyens took Gertrude Jekyll to Lindisfarne in May 1906 and, several years later in 1911, he designed the walls and paths inside the $83 \times 88 \times 67 \times 72$ft/ $25.3 \times 26.8 \times 20.4 \times 21.9$m walled garden to the north of the castle. Gertrude Jekyll also drew up planting plans for the garden in 1911. Her August plan shows roses, shrubs, perennials and annuals in her familiar drifts of colour, graduating from greys, blues and whites, through scarlets, pinks and oranges, to enliven the dullest of summer days. This garden, although small, was labour intensive like all of Jekyll's gardens. It is hard to imagine a more inhospitable place to create a garden—a flat, wind-swept, treeless site without water. The walls offered some protection, but hazel branches had to be brought across the causeway from the mainland to support many plants.

Over the years, the garden became neglected and overgrown, until 1972 when Dr Michael Tooley unearthed Gertrude Jekyll's plans in the Reef Point Garden Collection of Drawings in the School of Environmental Design, University of California, Berkeley. He persuaded The National Trust, who own Lindisfarne Castle, to let him lead a team of students from Durham University to restore the derelict garden. Once the weeds had been cleared away, the paths and outline of the original beds could be seen, as well as a few of Gertrude Jekyll's original plants. The replanting closely followed her plan, although some plants were no longer available and perennials replaced annuals; but over fifty of the plants she recommended can be seen in the garden today. Thrift and harebells have naturally self-seeded in the paths, their pastel-coloured flowers toning well with the introduced plants. The inner margins of the five central beds are bordered by grey-leaved lamb's tongue, *Stachys olympica*, known in Jekyll's time as *S. lanata*. This was a great favourite of hers and she also used it as a border plant in the Dutch Garden at Hestercombe.

Lutyens designed the garden to be viewed from the Ship Room where he often sat; it can also be seen from other north-facing windows. His idea of the distorted square was to make the garden appear larger from the castle than in reality. By slightly reducing the widths of paths and borders, the south–north and east–west lines were supposed to lead to vanishing points to the north and west respectively. However, by using a 1793 enclosure wall, Edwin Lutyens lost the illusion of size. Michael Tooley has calculated the desired effect can be seen only 'by hovering some 20ft/6m above the walls of the lower battery!'

Walled garden, Lindisfarne Castle from east bedroom window. 25 July 1986

A Foreground to a Vista

SUTTON PARK

A broad vista dotted with spinneys of mature trees cannot be created within a lifetime; so the splendid eighteenth-century vista from the south front, was a wonderful bonus for Major and Mrs Reginald Sheffield when they bought Sutton Park in Yorkshire in 1962. At this time, however, the architectural lines of the two terraces between the house and park were obscured by overgrown evergreens.

One of the first tasks was to uproot these shrubs. Most of the upper terrace was then grassed over, but outside the library, York stone flags, rescued from kitchens of old houses, were laid with wide gaps between them. This allowed the large expanse of flagstones to be softened with mounds of *Alchemilla mollis*, thyme, alpine phlox, and geraniums as well as spikes of *Sisyrinchium striatum* and *Verbascum phlomoides*. In the borders beneath the windows, Nancie Sheffield has scented plants such as *Nicotiana*, honeysuckle and *Lilium regale*, infilled with night-scented stock and apple mint *Mentha suaveolens*, so fragrant-scented air wafts in through open windows on a warm summer's evening.

The garden was extended 60ft/18m into the park—reputed by some to have been landscaped by 'Capability' Brown—so a fine cedar of Lebanon could be brought into the garden to give a feeling of maturity. The line of the beech hedge, planted to separate the park from the garden, was softened by a semicircular arc placed on the axis of the main vista. A large curving stone seat nestles inside the hedge, from where there is a fine view up the rising terraces towards the Georgian house. The opposite view from the house clearly shows one of the maxims of the garden designer Percy Cane: '... there should be no rival claims of formal and landscape styles'. He was commissioned to design the layout for the rose garden on the second terrace. Rectangular island beds, each with a willow-leafed pear *Pyrus salicifolia* pruned into a silvery umbrella, give a formal structure to the terrace, now informally planted with hybrid tea roses, delphiniums and other perennials. Old and shrub roses are planted in the east and west borders.

The lower, third terrace is the most formal. After it had been levelled, a lily canal was built to introduce a water feature to the garden. The far side of the rectangular canal extends outwards into an arc repeating the shape of the beech hedge beyond. A line of columnar *Chamaecyparis lawsoniana* 'Allumii', planted against the retaining wall of the second terrace, adds height and additional formality to the lower terrace. Every five years, scaffolding is erected for clipping the conifers.

The three terraces, although roughly equal in size, have a distinct design and associated planting. On each, a degree of formality is provided by regular lines, most obviously seen in the lower terrace with the canal. A photograph published in a 1975 issue of *Country Life*, shows the view from the house to be much more open than it is today, now that shrubs planted against the retaining wall of the first terrace obscure a clear view of the rose garden layout.

Nancie Sheffield, clearly adores her garden, adopting a wonderful philosophy since her husband died: 'I can never be lonely, because everywhere I see familiar faces in the plants given me by friends.' She particularly likes the early morning and late evening light when the shadows are long and scent is intoxicating.

Descending terraces and formal conifers with the park beyond the garden. 3 July 1987

A Romantic Vision

HEVER CASTLE

How familiar the views from the windows overlooking the drive of Hever Castle must have been to Anne Boleyn, as she waited for Henry VIII's visits during their courtship in 1530. Anne's happiness however, was shortlived, for her marriage lasted three brief years before she was beheaded; but her daughter Elizabeth eventually became queen. After Henry gave this Kent castle to his fourth wife, Anne of Cleeves, it slid into obscurity. By the time William Waldorf Astor, an American millionaire, set eyes on it in 1903, a succession of tenant farmers had let their geese and ducks loose on the moat, hung their hams from the ancient beams and stacked up corn and potatoes in the ground floor rooms. Still he fell in love with the site, bought the castle and set about restoring it and developing the gardens on a lavish scale. After he became a British citizen, he was created first Viscount Astor of Hever.

The farm buildings were demolished and a hundred-roomed Tudor village was built to house the kitchens, staff, and family as well as providing the guest rooms required by Lord Astor. Sited in a hollow, adjacent to the river Eden, Hever Castle was prone to flooding, so Lord Astor had the river realigned and dammed to create a 35-acre lake and a second moat was dug outside the original one. Full grown trees were transplanted from Ashdown Forest to create an instant mature landscape. Between the two moats, a series of more intimate and formal gardens were laid out, including a maze.

This elevated view from the castle shows part of the maze, planted in 1906 using a thousand yews. Measuring 80ft/24m square, the hedges are 8ft/2.4m high and the length of the internal pathways is a quarter of a mile long. Adjacent to the maze is Anne Boleyn's garden—a series of small gardens enclosed by yew hedges. The herb garden contains plants grown in her time, and the golden yew topiary chess pieces in the Chess Garden are based on designs found in the British Museum of pieces used during Henry VIII's reign. Abstract and animal topiary yew figures are a notable year-round feature of the driveway to the forecourt.

Beyond the maze, part of the outer moat can be seen and in the distance, stone buildings leading to the Italian Garden. Quite out of character with a Tudor castle, this garden was discretely tucked away behind high yew hedges. It was specifically designed to display the huge collection of Roman and Italian Renaissance antiquities bought by Lord Astor while he was American Ambassador to Italy from 1882–1885. A golden sandstone wall, known as the Pompeiian Wall, runs along the northern boundary where a galaxy of plants, notably climbers, festoon the columns, statues, sarcophagi and well-heads, enhancing and softening the stonework. A pergola, well clothed with climbers runs the length of the south boundary, and parallel to this is the grotto garden, inspired by the Wall of the Hundred Fountains at Villa d'Este near Rome. Lush growths of shade-loving mosses, ferns, hostas and primulas grow in profusion along this north-facing wall. Carpets of daffodils in Anne Boleyn's orchard, to the west of the castle, are a prelude to the ever-changing floral displays at Hever.

The combination of formal and informal styles, with architectural and living embellishments, has allowed a man to realize his vision on an historic site full of romantic memories.

An elevated view of part of the maze, moat and pergola. 16 June 1987

Complementing the Architecture

HESTERCOMBE GARDENS

Like so many historical gardens, Hestercombe House in Somerset has had its ups and downs. In 1750, Coplestone Warre Bampfylde wanted a picturesque landscape in the style of Henry Hoare's Stourhead in Wiltshire; and so the valley behind Hestercombe was transformed with lawns, trees, pools, cascades and even a temple. The house was later sold to Viscount Portman and in 1903 Edwin Lutyens was commissioned to design a garden adjacent to the house. Lutyens decided to exploit the splendid south-facing vista across the fields to the Vale of Taunton, by creating a series of terraces around a sunken garden. Three sides of the Great Plat were surrounded by walls of rough split stone quarried from behind the house, while the remaining side was bordered with an impressive 230ft/70m long pergola with alternating square and round slivered stone pillars. Lutyens' architectural design was complemented by Gertrude Jekyll's planting; together they created an Edwardian garden which befitted guests strolling at their leisure on a midsummer's day.

To offset death duties, the house and estate were sold by the Portman family to the Crown Commissioners in 1944, but the Hon Mrs E A B Portman continued to live in part of the house until she died in 1952. In the following year it was leased to the Somerset Fire Brigade for use as their headquarters. By then, much of the garden stonework was crumbling and most of the original planting had died and been replaced with plants not included in Jekyll's scheme. After some of her plans came to light in the potting shed and others were found in the Reef Point Collection (p24), a decision was made in 1973 to restore the garden. Photographs illustrating *Country Life* articles in 1908 and 1927, show the positioning of artefacts, auctioned in the early 1950s; but perhaps, more importantly they show that some planting changes were made to the original plans. All the crumbling stonework was replaced and the wooden cross beams of the pergola were once again made from Forest of Dean oaks. Plants no longer easily available were gleaned from diverse sources.

This picture shows two of the four flight of steps, with shallow risers and wide treads, leading down to the Great Plat. The beds are laid out symmetrically, edged with *Bergenia cordifolia* and filled with *Paeonia* 'Sarah Bernhardt', the floribunda rose 'Natalie Nypels', *Lilium regale*, the grass, *Miscanthus sinensis gracillimus* and delphiniums. The pergola columns are softened with vines, clematis and climbing roses and when the sun shines, a striking shadow pattern from the overhead timbers is cast on the paved walkway beneath.

The raised east terrace planted with warm colours can be seen overleaf. A dry narrow water course, known as a rill, runs the entire 140ft/42m length, but plans are under way to restore the water supply, as indeed, has already been achieved in the rill on the west terrace. At each end of the pergola the wall is perforated by three peep-holes allowing glimpses on to the fields beyond. Above the north end of the east rill is the rotunda—a circular walled area complete with pool. This functions as a pivot point for the walk leading to the orangery and Dutch garden beyond.

In 1978, Somerset County Council received a European Architectural Heritage Year Award for the restoration of this important garden by Lutyens and Jekyll.

OPPOSITE: *The Great Plat, pergola and borrowed vista beyond.* *7 July 1987*   OVERLEAF: *The east rill terrace.* *4 July 1986*

HISTORICAL ASPECTS

THE distinct periods in garden history, from Medieval times to the present day, have been extensively recorded elsewhere, so instead of giving a précis here, the style of each period is reflected by a glimpse through a window from that time.

A picture of a garden in the Middle Ages, has to be pieced together from scanty evidence gleaned from contemporary paintings and embroideries. A garden in the thirteenth-century style, known as Queen Eleanor's Garden after Eleanor of Provence and Eleanor of Castile, designed by Sylvia Landsberg and John Harvey was opened in 1986 adjacent to the Great Hall of Winchester Castle. It encompasses features known to have existed in royal gardens of that period when a trellis behind a turf seat was adorned with roses, the Queen's herber was covered with a living carpet of camomile and Madonna lilies scented the air. Elsewhere, copious wild flowers in cultivation adorned the garden.

By the time Henry VIII gazed down from his apartments, gardens had become much more elaborate—a large square area was divided into quarters and filled with patterns in the form of knots (p89). Mazes and other topiary forms remained popular during the Elizabethan era, when elevated views were also enjoyed by guests who gazed through expansive leaded-pane windows in the first floor long gallery.

The vogue for clipping evergreens led to even more elaborate designs appearing in seventeenth-century gardens. Fortunately, the topiary garden laid out at Levens Hall in Cumbria by Monsieur Beamont nearly three hundred years ago, still exists today. The overview from the upper windows of the Elizabethan mansion reveals the diversity of shapes—both geometric and naturalistic—of the green and golden yews contained in box-edged beds.

By the eighteenth century, the passion for pattern and formality, of topiary-lined axes creating vistas from the house, began to wane. As the landscape movement gathered strength, formal terraces and avenues were swept away. 'Capability' Brown created his idealized natural landscapes on a vast scale; expansive, undulating lawns planted with scattered clumps of trees, extended from the house towards a lake and beyond.

Colour returned to the garden early in the nineteenth century when Humphry Repton introduced formal flower beds. When Thomas L Fish bought Knowle Cottage at Sidmouth in Devon in 1820, he converted it into an 'Elegant Marine Villa Ornée' and in 1834, he published his *Guide to Illustrations and Views of Knowle Cottage, Sidmouth* for friends and visitors to the Devonshire resort. All the gothic-style windows on the south side of the house, looked out on to a Regency flower garden with circular basket beds. When the elegant full length drawing room windows were opened, the floriferous garden complete with peacocks, was viewed within the gothick frame.

Towards the latter part of the nineteenth century, elaborate carpet bedding designs, made from dwarf foliage plants, graced terraces near the house. Reminiscent of the way knots were hastily created before Elizabeth I visited a country mansion, it was not unknown for carpet bedding to be changed from one week to the next! Towards the turn of the century, the pendulum swung once again; William Robinson deplored carpet bedding and advocated informal planting later supported by Gertrude Jekyll (pp25, 32 and 43).

In this latter part of the twentieth century, the expanding interest in gardens and garden history has ensured historically important gardens such as Painshill (p39) and Hawkstone (p77) will be restored to their former glory.

A Tudor Revival

THE TUDOR GARDEN, SOUTHAMPTON

Adjacent to Southampton Water, hidden behind walls, a sixteenth-century style garden has been created by Sylvia Landsberg. Painstakingly, she pieced together evidence of garden features gleaned from texts, illustrations and paintings of the Tudor period to produce not a complete replica of a single garden; but a living, authenticated tableau of the varied facets to be seen in gardens at this time.

The centrepiece is a knot based on a design taken from *La Maison Rustique* (1582) and a similar pattern can be seen carved on the hall doors of Tudor House. Indeed, many of the knots created at this time were adapted from designs originally carved in wood or embroidered on fabrics. The Southampton knot which measures 15½ft/4.7m square, is bordered with cotton lavender *Santolina chamaecyparissus*; inside, intertwining straps of winter savory *Satureia montana*, wall germander *Teucrium chamaedrys* and box are infilled with gravel. The knot was planted in 1980 for the opening of the Tudor Garden in July of the following year. It was replanted in 1985 and the *Santolina* edging replanted a year later. Between April and September, the knot is clipped every three to four weeks.

Bordering the knot are rectangular and L-shaped beds filled, like the whole Tudor garden, with plants typical of sixteenth-century gardens. Many are British wild plants, grown, not just to bring colour to the garden, or for bordering beds like thrift *Armeria maritima*, but also for specific culinary or medicinal uses; plants such as comfrey *Symphytum officinale* (for bruises); lungwort *Pulmonaria officinalis* (for lung diseases); orris *Iris germanica* (used cosmetically) and the gladdon *Iris foetidissima* (for drawing out thorns). In Tudor times it was perfectly legal to gather any wild plant from the countryside. Other plants of ancient origin, such as pot marigold *Calendula officinalis* (for dyeing hair and for salads) and elecampane *Inula helenium* (for sciatica) would have been swapped with friends and neighbours, as indeed, so many plants are introduced to gardens today.

Among the other features in the Tudor Garden are herb beds—these had to be narrow enough so that weeders could reach the centre from the surrounding sand paths—a fountain, an arbour and a parapet looking out on to Southampton Water. There is also a small secret garden which is visible through two peep-holes in a bay hedge. On the far side is a bee bole, complete with skep, protected with a miniature thatched roof; other skeps are shielded by a wattle stand.

The range of plants grown in Tudor Gardens was very limited, consequently royal gardens were embellished with architectural features such as striped railings and poles. The design of the poles, topped with heraldic beasts and railings in the Southampton garden, originated from poles portrayed in a blinkered view through a window in the background of a painting by an unknown artist of *The Family of Henry VIII* c1545. Henry's courtiers certainly used heraldic emblems and Tudor House was occupied from 1520 by Sir Richard Lyster, the Lord Chief Justice of England, who would have been familiar with the Hampton Court gardens.

There can be no better way of appreciating the more desirable aspects of life in Tudor times than to experience this imaginative and unique outdoor living museum, designed for Southampton City Council.

Herb knot in Tudor Garden with striped poles flanking the arbour behind. 4 August 1986

A Seventeenth Century Design

MOSELEY OLD HALL

Few people as they skirt Wolverhampton on the M54 or M6 motorways, probably appreciate they are passing near an historic site and a delightful garden. Moseley Old Hall was one of several houses where King Charles II arrived, disguised as a woodman, to take refuge after his defeat in the Battle of Worcester in 1651. When the house and gardens were given to The National Trust in 1962, pigsties, hen-runs and fragmented glass cloches unceremoniously filled the one-acre garden. With great imagination, a garden in the seventeenth-century style was created, filled only with those plants known to have been cultivated at this time.

The most distinctive part of the garden is the knot, laid out on the west side of the house. Based on one of four designs created by the Reverend Walter Stonehouse in 1640, it is made simply from dwarf box *Buxus sempervirens* 'Suffruticosa', pebbles and two different coloured gravels. Each of the eleven repeating patterns comprises four box-edged shapes filled with purple gravel around a circular box bed covered with grey pebbles and a standard mop head box in the centre. The trunks of the standard box are strengthened by stakes and protected against rabbit damage by wire mesh. Beige gravel covers the paths round the beds, so that the whole effect is of green shapes set against neutral-toned backgrounds. The knot is maintained by raking the gravel when necessary and clipping the box twice a year. The pattern of the entire knot garden is best appreciated from an upper floor window in the house. Running along the entire length of one side of the knot is a wooden arbour with many arched windows overlooking the formal garden. The design of the arbour is taken from Thomas Hill's *A Gardener's Labyrinth* (1577). Two fragrant clematis, the virgin's bower *C. flammula* and *C. viticella* were among the relatively few climbing plants cultivated during the seventeenth century. *C. viticella* is now flowering on the wooden arbour, together with the claret vine *Vitis vinifera* 'Purpurea' but *C. flammula* is unfortunately not thriving and replacements are proving difficult to obtain. The arbour walk, banked with English lavender *Lavandula angustifolia*, leads via a hornbeam tunnel to a nut walk at the far end of the knot. Different varieties of hazel have been planted along the nut walk opening out into an orchard where old-fashioned fruit trees—mulberries, quinces, medlars and Morello cherries—have been planted.

Elsewhere, old cottage garden plants are cultivated, such as the sweet smelling Madonna lily *Lilium candidum*, red valerian *Centranthus ruber* and the double-flowered soapwort *Saponaria officinalis*. If crushed soapwort leaves and roots are boiled, the strained liquid will make a lather. Proof of its use in ancient times as a washing plant comes from the medieval name Foam Dock and today the mildness of soapwort is infinitely preferable to modern soaps for cleaning ancient tapestries. European settlers in New England took the plant with them, discovering that the soapy water helped to relieve the painful rash caused by poison ivy *Rhus radicans*.

Several roses, including the musk rose *Rosa moschata*, the eglantine rose *Rosa arvensis*, the white rose of York *Rosa* × *alba* and the red rose of Lancaster *Rosa gallica officinalis* also embellish this small, but fascinating National Trust garden. The living green knot remains a feature that can be appreciated all year round.

An elevated view of the knot garden created from box and gravels. 2 July 1987

A Picturesque Landscape

PAINSHILL PARK

The transformation of a barren tract of Surrey heathland into one of the finest English eighteenth-century landscape parks, required considerable foresight. The Hon Charles Hamilton provided the inspiration. Like all young nobility and gentry of his day, he made the Grand Tour to the Continent, ending with a two-year spell in Rome, where he took up painting and began to collect paintings and statues. After a second trip to Rome, he conceived the idea of creating a three-dimensional landscape on a grand scale.

Not being a rich man, Hamilton borrowed money between 1737–8 to purchase and lease initially some 200 acres of land at Painshill near Cobham. Here he began to develop his ornamental pleasure grounds surrounded by a crescent of open parkland with clumps of trees, shortly before Henry Hoare II began work on Stourhead in 1743. Hamilton's aim was to create a series of unexpected pictures, a mixture of open and closed vistas, so that visitors walking the tortuous circuit, would lose all feeling of time and place. Even Horace Walpole was impressed, for in 1748 he wrote: 'Mr Hamilton has really made a fine place out of a most cursed hill.'

Nothing daunted Hamilton, for example he installed a water wheel to pump up water from the river Mole to fill the 14-acre lake. He developed a great interest in horticulture and planted many recently introduced exotic conifers at Painshill. When Charles von Linné, son of the Swedish botanist Linnaeus, saw Painshill in 1781, he commented he had never before seen such a large variety of fir trees. After the major landscaping was complete, between 1758–62 Hamilton had six follies erected: a Gothic Temple, the Mausoleum, a Turkish Tent, the Temple of Bacchus, the Hermitage and the Gothic Tower. The Turkish Tent and the Hermitage have long since disappeared, but the Temple of Bacchus foundations have been excavated. A grotto by Josiah Lane was completed in 1765 using lightweight limestone tufa for the outside. The interior was lined with artificial crystals and stalactites, illuminated by sunlight reflected from the lake, shining through apertures in the walls.

Other great contemporary landscapes at Stourhead, Hagley and Bowood, belonged to Charles Hamilton's friends, on whom he presumably exerted some influence. He certainly designed the informal cascade at Bowood and the Turkish Tent was added to Stourhead after Hamilton had secured a loan from Hoare in 1766.

Hamilton spent over thirty years developing his park, but was then forced to sell up to repay his debts. There was a succession of private owners until in 1948 the park was sold off in lots. Elmbridge Borough Council gradually bought up the land until by 1980 they had acquired 158 of the 250 acres. In 1981 the Painshill Park Trust was set up to restore the landscape park and surviving buildings. Extensive initial surveys were conducted, paths were cleared and tree surgeons employed—a hundred and sixty-nine of Hamilton's original trees, notably some huge cedars, survive. The Gothic Temple with its fan vaulted ceiling was restored in 1985 and, after extensive shrub clearance, the first historic vista (shown here) down from the Temple to the lake below was restored. It is hoped Painshill will soon be open on a regular basis, so that new generations of visitors will learn to appreciate one of the earliest and finest examples of landscape parks in England.

*View through restored
windows in Gothic
Temple to vista with the
lake below.
8 June 1987*

A Circular Carpet

NATIONAL BOTANIC GARDENS, DUBLIN

The art of bedding out dwarf plants into intricate designs reminiscent of carpets, first appeared in the British Isles at the end of the 1860s and remained fashionable in private gardens for two decades. Some of the best carpet bedding designs seen in London parks in 1875 are illustrated in the 1881 edition of Robert Thompson's *The Gardener's Assistant*. Known as *mosaïculture* in Europe, carpet bedding was created by the dense planting of dwarf foliage plants of contrasting colours, in the form of a mosaic or a geometrical design. Later designs incorporated zoomorphic figures. Sometimes, dwarf flowering plants were used, so a wider range of colours was achieved.

By the end of the last century, William Robinson's positive distaste for formal planting and his active crusade for more natural and informal planting, later supported by Gertrude Jekyll, led to carpet beds disappearing from private gardens, although they were still seen in public parks. Floral clocks with outsized numerals and hands, or emblems depicting an anniversary, are produced annually in some British and French parks, but they are a poor substitute for the artistic creations of the last century.

One of the few places where a traditional carpet bedding design, planted with succulents, can still be seen is in the National Botanic Gardens at Glasnevin in Dublin. Each summer, two circular beds just inside the main entrance have been planted, virtually unchanged, for about forty years. The simple design incorporates an eight-armed star, representing the compass points, inside a scalloped motif. Over the years, there has been a slight variation in the size of the star, so now wooden templates are used to define the stars and the scalloping.

Using *Kleinia repens*, *Echeveria elegans*, *E. glauca*, *Crassula cooperi* and *C. schmidtii*, a delightful harmonious blending of blue-green, pink and red blocks of colour is achieved. At the end of May, when the impact of the spring bedding has faded, the pansies and tulips are lifted and a 3in/7.5cm layer of fine granite sand from the Wicklow Mountains is spread over each bed. A small *Yucca aloifolia* 'Variegata' is planted as the centre plant and then it takes two people about a fortnight to plant approximately ten thousand plants in a single bed. Both species of *Echeveria* are overwintered in trays under glass and each plant has its roots removed before planting. Larger specimens will also have their outer leaves removed, because the best effect is produced by using rosettes of a uniform size. For almost a quarter of a century, Walter Murphy has planted out the circular beds; in 1987 he was assisted by Mary Reape. They work from a wooden plank raised on blocks above the bed, using wooden dibbers. As the plants grow and fill the small gaps around them, very little weeding is required, but if the colour blocks are to be maintained any flowering spikes which appear must be pinched out. Towards the end of the summer, the colours of the *Echeveria* in particular, are enriched. At the first hint of a frost, all the plants are lifted and retained for replanting in the following spring.

In recent years, the restoration and, indeed, creation of many knots and parterres, has reawakened interest in formal garden design. Maybe these attractive beds at Glasnevin will inspire a limited revival of traditionally styled carpet bedding in other public gardens?

Succulents planted out in a Victorian-style carpet bedding design. 18 August 1987

Renascence of a Jekyll Garden

When a large Edwardian house in Hampshire came up for sale in 1983, the prospective buyers had not even heard of Gertrude Jekyll. They were, however, intrigued to discover why the property should have been listed as being of historical significance. Their researches revealed the 4-acre garden had been designed by Jekyll in 1908. After Rosamund Wallinger obtained copies of the original plans held in the Reef Point Collection in California, she was determined to restore the gardens to their former glory.

To the rear of the house, the plans showed a pergola with a catenary of hanging ropes as supports for a variety of climbing plants. The path beneath the pergola led down to a sunken rose garden bordered by stone walls—one side structurally the mirror image of the other. The central feature in each half was a stepped square stone bed.

By 1983, the garden had become an overgrown wilderness and many of the original features were indiscernible. Four days with a mechanical excavator and many bonfires did wonders, revealing the remains of the stone walls and original beds. The walls were rebuilt using the old stones, and plants, dormant for some sixty years, sprouted anew—plants such as hart's tongue ferns *Phyllitis scolopendrium* and *Campanula carpatica*. The next task was to decipher Jekyll's spidery handwriting so that the plants she specified could be listed as several of the names had changed since Edwardian times. The Hampshire Gardens Trust, founded in 1984 to stimulate an interest in the county's gardens, endorsed an application for a grant from Hampshire County Council. This enabled Penelope Hobhouse, the garden planning consultant, to advise on the replanting, mostly done in 1985–6 with additions in 1986–7. Wherever possible, Rosamund Wallinger has tried to use the plants specified on the plans. Several old irises prone to disease are no longer in cultivation, so modern cultivars with similar coloured flowers have been substituted. When 'Madame Caroline Testout' roses were ordered from Peter Beales' rose nursery, they turned out to be climbers, whereas Jekyll had specified shrub roses for the central beds. Quite by chance, in the 1986 summer, Peter Beales visited a girls' boarding school where there was a tradition for parents to give a rose as their daughter's leaving present. He spotted a bush form of 'Madame Caroline Testout' planted in the 1920s, but it will be several years before he has stock for sale.

Some weeks before the pink roses open, *Paeonia* 'Sarah Bernhardt' produces its pale pink flowers. *Lilium regale* in the central beds, unusually planted in pots as clearly specified on the plans, are to be replaced by *L. longiflorum* for 1988. The beds are edged with *Stachys olympica*, which Jekyll also used for the Lindisfarne garden (p25). Both this intimate Hampshire garden and the Great Plat at Hestercombe (p30) were designed to reach their peak in midsummer with white lilies and pink roses in flower. Later, the emphasis shifts to yellows and reds in the raised beds flanking the sunken garden.

Rosamund Wallinger's achievements, with only a few hours' assistance a week, should be an inspiration to anyone contemplating the restoration of a neglected historic garden. She is now restoring Jekyll's wild garden and pond at the front of the house, to complete the renascence of an early twentieth-century garden.

Raised stone bed with potted lilies. 9 July 1987

Elevated view looking through Irish yews to the gothick summerhouse. 28 July 1987

A Twentieth Century Transformation

BARNSLEY HOUSE

Some people might prefer to design a garden from scratch, rather than transform a well-established garden. Rosemary Verey has no doubt that when she and her husband inherited Barnsley House in Gloucestershire in 1951, they were most fortunate in acquiring Cotswold stone walls built in 1770, fine old trees planted about 1850 and an eighteenth-century gothick summerhouse as the 'bones' on which they could build their ideas. But it was a decade later, after the children had finished playing on the lawns, that work began on transforming the garden. David Verey's architectural skills, perfectly complemented his wife's knowledge of plants and garden history. Together they introduced hidden features and vistas, blending formality and informality to produce an internationally renowned garden.

The Cotswold stone path leading from the drawing room door bordered by Irish yews planted in 1948, was enlivened with rock roses. This view, from an upper window in Rosemary Verey's new house (her eldest son Charles and his family moved into the main house in 1988) looks between the yews to mixed borders and the gothick summerhouse beyond. The holm oak is one of the original 1850 specimen trees. An early 1960s feature was the 'wilderness' area, planted with trees providing attractive spring blossom and glowing autumn colours. Mown paths meander through the uncut grass carpeted with spring bulbs. The vista down a pleached lime walk with a pebble pathway, was later extended with a laburnum walk underplanted with *Allium aflatunense*.

The Tuscan temple was moved from nearby Fairford Park and resited at Barnsley as an eyecatcher at one end of a long vista. In front of the temple is a pond, beyond which nineteenth-century iron gates open on to a grass broadwalk leading to a fountain designed by Simon Verity. Water plays from the mouths of four frogs on to flat spangled Purbeck stone carved in relief to represent two Cotswold stone rams, and drips from a Horton stone plinth into a small pool below.

In winter, sheets of snowdrops and winter aconites are succeeded by clumps of stinking hellebores *Helleborus foetidus* flowering under trees along the main drive. Later, the dying leaves of spring bulbs in beds beyond the flagged patio are ingeniously camouflaged by the new growth of hardy perennials. In front of the castellated verandah, a knot garden was laid out in 1975 and the interlacing threads infilled with gravel. One of the seventeenth-century designs is a lover's knot of interwoven box, while the other is a mixed planting of box, wall germander *Teucrium chamaedrys* and *Phillyrea angustifolia*. Most herb gardens are dull in winter; but at Barnsley the diamond pattern of the box hedge is attractive long after the herbs have died down.

The potager, laid out in designs adapted from William Lawson's *Country Housewife's Garden*, admirably demonstrates that growing vegetables need not be dull. A formal design of old brick paths is interplanted with vegetables and fruit trees grown in a decorative way; apple trees are trained as espaliers and goblets, while runner beans climb over arches forming a tunnel.

With the recent addition of a new conservatory, the garden continues to evolve. Barnsley blends formal design with informal planting, to produce a garden so varied in design, that many visits throughout the year are required to appreciate it fully.

ARCHITECTURAL FEATURES

ITALIANS place much greater emphasis on architecture in gardens than either the British or Americans; yet all use garden buildings, statues, walls, pools and pathways to provide permanent frameworks for more transitory plants. The permanence of living sculpture in the form of topiary depends on how well it is maintained. Topiary which has lasted for several centuries includes the Monasterio de San Lorenzo in Spain (p57), the topiary gardens at Levens Hall in Cumbria and at the medieval Castello Balduino at Montalto de Pavia high up in the Apennines. Garden furniture and plant containers are a way of introducing contrasting colour and texture to a garden which can be moved around to suit the changing seasons.

Individual statues can be framed within an aperture, like the discus thrower, seen through the bull's eye window at Polesden Lacey in Surrey, or placed at the end of an allée or in a vista framed by an avenue of trees. At Brookgreen Gardens in South Carolina, a gilded bronze statue of Dionysus by Edward McCartan, is a radiant focal point at the end of the avenue of live oaks, dripping with Spanish moss, whether seen spot lit by sun or the soft light on a cloudy day. The gardens were begun in 1931 by Archer Huntingdon, as an outdoor museum for exhibiting the work of American sculptors—including that of his wife Anna Hyatt Huntingdon—as well as for preserving the indigenous flora and fauna of this part of South Carolina. By April 1987, the Gardens contained 451 statues of figures and animals, each embellished by positioning in a harmonious native floral setting.

Numerous statues, fountains and cascades are all part of Le Blond's grand vista stretching out below the north front of Peterhof (Petrodvorets)—Peter the Great's summer palace outside Leningrad. Water jets playing on the gilded statues ensure they glisten in all kinds of weather.

Windows in garden buildings and follies can be used to frame distant vistas or focal points such as a tree, a colourful planting or a water feature. Windows in hedges enclosing a garden room are not uncommon, but windows cut into both sides of a topiary tunnel or arbour are a forgotten art. A Flemish embroidery c1590 and a Dutch painting c1620, depict windows in arbours and tunnels which surround a moated garden, allowing views both on to the enclosed garden and across the moat. Early in the seventeenth century, John James in his *Theory and Practice of Gardening*, shows an engraving of a type of palisade as a clipped green wall punctuated by many tall, arched windows.

Tall architectural features cast shadows which break up the expanse of uniformly toned paths or patios. Simple repetitive shadows are cast by rows of linear columns, statues and fastigiate trees—notably the columnar funeral cypresses so popular in south European gardens. The supports and cross beams of a pergola cast simple shadow patterns on a large scale; more elaborate patterns on a smaller scale are cast by the Spanish *rejas* or grilles and Chinese latticework on pavements and courtyards. Rejas and lattice windows also give views of the garden beyond the wall (p124). Enclosed seventeenth-century British gardens allowed glimpses of the landscape outside, via an open wrought iron panel set into a wall—a form of *clair-voyée*.

A view from a window into a small walled garden can be greatly enhanced by placing a mirror to reflect hidden views. If the mirror is mounted on the wall within a trellis framework, it then appears as a window in a wall with a vista beyond. A *trompe l'oeil* painting on a wall of a distant view is another clever device for creating an impression of a view through a window in a confined space.

Shapes & Shadows

PARNHAM HOUSE

Parnham House is a magnificent Tudor manor in Dorset surrounded by formal and informal gardens laid out at different times during this century. The house dates from 1540 but in 1810 John Nash, the Regency architect, added castellations as well as gothick windows and ceilings. When Hans Sauer bought Parnham a century later, he stripped out the gothick ceilings, reinstated the Tudor interiors and replaced the windows with small leaded panes.

Sauer also had the gardens landscaped—probably by Inigo Thomas, who laid out the garden at nearby Athelhampton, including the huge pyramidal yews. A walled forecourt was built at the east-facing front and a series of three terraces on the south side. Next to the house is the expansive balustraded Ladies Terrace flanked by a pair of gazebos, at one time used as aviaries. One of these gazebos is depicted, complete with parrot and a thieving jackdaw, in the *trompe l'oeil* painted in 1932 by Talbot Hughes RA on the wall beside the William and Mary staircase in the house. Balustrated steps lead down to the Yew Tree Terrace where fifty conical yews line two squares surrounding the sunken lawns. Between the central lines of yews run two stone rills fed by a spring issuing from a lion's head fountain in the wall of the balustrade. At the end of each rill, water cascades down a staircase into an underground channel leading to the river Brit along the western boundary.

When John Makepeace bought Parnham in 1976, the house had been empty for three years and the gardens were much neglected. His wife, Jennie, has been the inspiration behind the restoration and planting programme. She confesses, 'It is impossible to find a gardener who is both a wizard with machines and a plantsman. Because we are so dependent on equipment for the weekly mowing of eight acres of lawns, I appointed Jeremy Burgess—a genius with machines—as the full-time gardener. With a part-time assistant, he also clips all the topiary and does the maintenance work, while I take care of the planning, planting and pruning.' After the formal Yew Terraces were restored, informal plantings were laid out, including a herb border. There is a Dutch Garden with silver, white and variegated plants, and an Iris Garden which glows with colour in June. In the Italian Garden, one border has soft blues, mauves, pinks and whites, another warm yellows, bronzes, oranges and reds.

Restoration continues—lawns on the Ladies Terrace and the front courtyard are being enlarged to their original proportions. Strips of keruing, a weather-resistant hardwood, will help to maintain the lawn edges. The next task is to restore the leaking rills.

This view of the Yew Tree Terrace is from Jennie Makepeace's favourite room, where she can find a moment of peace from the constant activity associated with The Parnham Trust and the School for Craftsmen in Wood, founded by John Makepeace in 1977. A decade later, the School for Woodland Industry was founded nearby at Hooke Park, with the aim of utilizing forest thinnings, normally burnt or pulped, in innovative construction techniques. At the entrance, a pair of brushwood sculptures by Andy Goldsworthy stand like two huge rustic moon gates framing woodland views. These ephemeral windows are in complete contrast to the permanent mullioned windows of the house.

Conical yews cast long shadows across the lawns early in the morning. 11 June 1987

A Luminous Window

DINMORE MANOR

The manufacture of highly decorative stained glass windows became feasible after two important discoveries were made. The first, nearly a thousand years ago, was the production of transparent coloured glass made by mixing metallic oxides with molten glass. The second advance came when narrow grooved lead strips replaced the rigid wood or hard metal framework for supporting glass panes; thereby allowing much more fluid shapes to be incorporated into the window design. Magnificent stained glass windows exist in churches and cathedrals, but even on a reduced scale, they can be most effective in apertures of enclosed caverns or grottoes, as once seen at Hawkstone (p76).

The colours of a stained glass window are enhanced when viewed surrounded by a dark aperture as in the grotto at Dinmore Manor in Hereford and Worcester. The grotto leads off from an octagonal court functioning as the pivot point for two rows of cloisters running at right angles to each other. The west-facing gothic-shaped window is viewed through a concave non-reflecting Perspex window and when the sun shines late in the day, the vivid colours of a mid-Eastern landscape—complete with palms and setting sun—are repeated in one of the small pools below the window. The horizon in the window design is ingeniously positioned to coincide with the true horizon outside. A rustic finish to the grotto interior was achieved by pressing concrete, mixed with realistic earth colours, through chicken wire. With great economy, any water which is surplus to domestic needs, is channelled into a circular lily pool in the garden, from where it overflows to feed the grotto pools before passing beneath the cloisters back to the rock garden.

In an attempt to keep ivies alive inside the grotto, lit only by a small upper window, one end of a felt strip has been planted alongside each plant and the other dipped into the pool to induce self-watering by capillary action. The system works well only in humid weather but not, when it is most needed, during dry periods.

From the twelfth to the sixteenth century, the site was the headquarters of the military and monastic order known as the Knights Hospitaller. Dinmore was one of the most important of some fifty Commanderies in England and Wales run by retired knights as a place for injured or invalided colleagues to recuperate, as well as for providing military training. A Commandery also provided shelter and food for passing travellers. Unlike the rest of the Manor which dates back to the late sixteenth century, the cloisters and grotto, together with the music room, were built after Richard Hollins Murray, the inventor of cats-eyes (reflecting lenses defining the mid-line of roads) bought Dinmore in 1927. Murray's additions in the early 1930s are a tribute to the days when the knights occupied Dinmore. The entire length of the west wall of the cloisters is enclosed and decorated with eight stained glass windows made by William Morris (Westminster) Limited. Like the much larger grotto windows, these glow strongly late in the day, and when the sun shines directly through them, the flagstones are painted with multi-coloured pools of light.

The view into the grotto illustrates how the juxtaposition of a stained glass window and water can produce a most striking and colourful year-round feature inside an enclosed space completely lacking living colour.

Permanent colour of stained glass grotto window repeated in a pool. 8 May 1987

An Elevated Viewpoint

STONE HOUSE COTTAGE GARDENS

With considerable forethought and a great deal of energy, James and Louisa Arbuthnott, in little more than a decade, have transformed a two-up two-down gardener's cottage in Worcestershire into their family home and a three-quarter-acre derelict garden into a plantsman's haven. Photographs taken in 1974 show the bricked walled garden, formerly the kitchen garden of a Georgian house, as a completely barren yard with the remnants of an old glasshouse.

Before any planting was done, the basic geometry of the garden design was planned on paper. To create the illusion of a much larger area, the garden was subdivided into a series of small compartments. Yew hedges planted in 1975–6 function both as internal living walls and as breaks for wind blowing off the Malvern Hills. From the south-east gate, three radiating paths flanked by yew hedges entice the visitor to enter and explore the garden. Openings through the hedges allow optional diversions to be made. The layout of the whole design is best appreciated from the elevated viewpoints of four brick towers gradually built by James Arbuthnott.

Once the compartments had been defined and the lawns laid down, beds were made for planting the rich assortment of unusual herbaceous plants, some grouped by their colour into separate white and yellow gardens; others into seasonal winter and spring gardens. Unquestionably, the speciality of Stone House Cottage Gardens is the plethora of wall shrubs and climbers. Every inch of the old walls has been exploited and a wooden pergola has recently been built to increase the growing area for climbing plants. Among the more spectacular are the rose 'Cooper's Burmese', *Bignonia capreolata*, *Lonicera tragophylla* and *Jasminum officinale* 'Argento-variegatum'.

Throughout the garden, other microhabitats have been created. Adjacent to the house, the brick foundations of the old glasshouse were made into raised beds; while old wooden railway sleepers were used to make a triangular-shaped bed for choice rock plants. Tucked away, outside one of the boundary walls is a north-east facing raised peat bed for shade-loving plants.

Many of the less hardy plants grown outside without any protection, have survived two severe winters, although there were some losses. Each September, potash is sprinkled around the most susceptible plants, to increase their tolerance of frost. In 1981–2, the temperature plunged to −26°C at Stone, yet many of the tender plants survived—the walls were clearly providing additional protection and warmth. Adjacent to the garden is a nursery, from where plants can be taken to replace the losses.

All the plants in the garden are labelled and comparatively few are repeated in this showcase for the nursery. Before purchases are made, the form and habitat of a plant can be checked as well as hints gained for associated planting. The summer months involve maintaining the garden, escorting visitors and selling plants; come the winter, Louisa plans next year's propagation on the computer, while James tackles the bricklaying.

The four towers, built into the outer walls, together give a clear overview of the garden, graphically illustrating how an elevated viewpoint brings a completely new perspective to a naturally flat side. The two- and three-storeyed towers also extend the vertical space available for especially vigorous climbers.

'Cooper's Burmese' rose frames a window in one tower which looks out to a second tower. 18 June 1987

A Gentleman's Folly

CASTLE TOR

The elevated garden of Castle Tor in the Devonshire resort of Torquay, has a magnificent south-facing seaward aspect, but the precipitous gradient below must have daunted many an owner. In the late 1920s Horace Pickersgill commissioned the Totness architect Frederick Harrild, a pupil of Edwin Lutyens, to landscape the garden. From c1928–34 an imaginative architectural design, reminiscent of Lutyens' style, was constructed from Somerset limestone, encompassing a series of terraces, a canal, tower and battlemented gatehouse complete with portcullis.

On the west side, steps and paths weave figures of eight through circular archways and around 6ft/2m diameter wall-mounted circular windows. From the top of the steps, the view through the two circles to the sea beyond is breathtaking and on some nights the reflection of the full moon appears within the frames. Windows are important features at Castle Tor: they are elongated in the orangery, narrow in the tower, and cruciform arrow-slits in the battlemented walls.

An impressive 20ft/6m retaining wall backs on to the main terrace dominated by a 120ft/36m long canal. At the west end, a cherub's mouth spouts water into the canal copiously planted with water lilies, bogbean *Menyanthes trifoliata* and the oxygenating plant *Elodea*. The present owner, Leonard Stocks, plans to find an ornamental heron to deter live herons from poaching the fish. Crossing the canal are circular stepping stones at one end and rectangular stone islands at the other. A pair of wall-mounted dolphin fountains on the orangery feed a series of terraced basins emptying into the canal. Another fountain plays from a central vegetated island

so the sound of running water is heard everywhere on this terrace. On the seaward edge, are yews clipped as topiary birds and a pair of helter-skelters. Twice a year, Leonard Stocks uses hand shears to shape the topiary and scissors to trim the delicate beaks. He has introduced many statues throughout the garden, particularly to enliven grassed areas originally broken up by flower beds. At the eastern end of the terrace is a stone tower commanding fine views across Lyme Bay to the east and across Tor Bay to the south.

A vivacious octogenarian neighbour, Dolly Kerr, recalls seeing the garden gradually develop. 'Horace Pickersgill spent all day working in the garden in such old clothes, he was often mistaken for the gardener. Castle Tor became known locally as Pickersgill's Folly, and nearby Castle Drogo [commissioned by Julius Drewe and built by Edwin Lutyens during the years 1911–1930] as Drewe's Folly.' It is more than likely that Pickersgill knew the terraced garden at Castle Drogo which possibly inspired him to landscape Castle Tor. He had always intended to leave the house and gardens to the town, but died unexpectedly in Bavaria.

A succession of subsequent owners had plenty of money but no great interest in the garden—one owner removed the *Cupressus macrocarpa* hedges because they scratched his Rolls Royce! In 1982, planning permission was given for a bungalow to be built on the terraces below the canal, and after even more ambitious developments were proposed, the garden and its buildings were listed by the Department of the Environment, thus halting all development. Leonard Stocks hopes one day to incorporate the lower terraces again.

Tor Bay seen through a pair of descending circular apertures. 16 August 1987

Allegorical Shapes

MONASTERIO DE SAN LORENZO
DE TRASSOUTO

In the Middle Ages, pilgrims came from all over Europe to Santiago de Compostela in Galicia, the north-western province of Spain, to see the shrine of St James the Greater. According to legend, this apostle journeyed across seas to convert Spain to Christianity. Nowadays, many visitors come to appreciate the Romanesque cathedral dating back to the eleventh century with the later baroque façade, but when the feast day of St James (25 July) falls on a Sunday, two million visitors pour in to see the shrine. Fronting on to the cathedral square is the Hostal de los Reyes Catolicos with its cloistered gardens (p.17), with formal shapes made from clipped box.

But the most intriguing of all the enclosed gardens in this romantic city is hidden away behind the high walls of the Monasterio de San Lorenzo de Trassouto. This small monastery was dedicated to San Lorenzo in 1216 by the Bishop of Zamora. In the fifteenth century, when it was owned by the Count of Altamira, the monastery was occupied by monks of the Franciscan order, where they remained for four centuries until the monastery was eventually taken over by the state. The Duquesa de Medina de las Torres, great grandmother of the present owner, the Duquesa de Soma, negotiated with the state for her family to regain ownership.

Inside the monastery is a chapel which contains a magnificent sixteenth-century marble altar piece and sepulchres brought by the Duquesa de Medina de las Torres from the church of San Francisco in Seville, which also belonged to the family. Just beyond the entrance to the chapel is a doorway leading to a courtyard which encloses the smallest part of the garden. It is filled with an almost solid 13ft/4m high mass of box topiary clipped into designs which are reputed to date back some four centuries. From the cloister at ground level it is difficult to appreciate fully the intricacy of the designs, but there are excellent views through the glazed windows of the first floor gallery around all four sides of the courtyard. The shapes include both allegorical and religious designs, among them alpha and omega and the grille of San Lorenzo. The Director of the Pontevedra Museum, José Filgueira Valverde, observes that the patterns, including the Maltese Cross and the shell of St James, are identical to some very old moulds used for making *flores*, a kind of pastry typical of the region.

When the Duquesa was asked how the topiary, with the very narrow spaces between the shapes, was clipped, she replied, with a twinkle in her eye, 'By a very thin man!' In fact, it is clipped twice a year—in November and May–June using narrow steps inside the topiary. Access to the top is gained by a man lying on a ladder from where he uses long-handled shears. In the centre of the garden, on the west side, a stone staircase leads down to a fountain, fed by natural spring water which plays on to a fifteenth-century statue of the Virgin.

Green tends to be the dominant colour in Spanish gardens; whether it be produced by box, yew, or cypresses, it no doubt compensates for the predominantely brown shades found in the natural arid landscapes of the central Spanish plateau. The garden beyond the cloister now contains cedars, araucarias, rhododendrons and camellias. It was here that the Franciscan monks used to meditate as they strolled along the paths in their walled retreat.

Ancient topiary shapes fill the cloisters of the San Lorenzo Monastery. 29 March 1987

An Italian Style

IFORD MANOR

Harold A Peto, the architect and garden designer, was attracted to the spectacular location of Iford Manor nestling in a secluded valley overlooking the river Frome where Wiltshire, Somerset and Avon meet. He must have had considerable foresight to see the potential of a garden with dense hanging woods above laurel thickets but he was fortunate in inheriting some fine plane and beech trees, planted a century before by Dr Thomas Gaisford.

After Peto cleared the scrub from the lower steep slopes and infilled the Victorian flower beds, he set about replacing the grass banks with a series of walled terraces using the old stone from the disused local bridleway. From 1899–1914, he landscaped the precipitous site, so he could put into practice his belief that a garden could attain the highest development of beauty only if architecture and plants were blended together. Here, at last, he had found a house and garden for displaying the Greek, Roman, Byzantine and Gothic antiquities collected on his European travels. The upper colonnaded great terrace runs 250ft/86m across the garden. Peto moved an eighteenth-century octagonal tea house from the mount in the kitchen garden to one end of the great terrace, building a Spanish-style *casita* at the other. Natural springs were tapped to feed a series of pools and a winding rill. Vistas were opened by felling twelve hundred trees, so gradually the sylvan garden was transformed into an Italianate masterpiece. Peto's last and most ambitious scheme was building the Italian-style cloisters.

After Peto's death in 1933 his nephew, Sir Michael Peto, lived at Iford for thirty years. Shortly afterwards, Elizabeth Cartwright fell in love with Iford, buying it in 1965. She has been restoring it and the unique garden ever since, enthusiastically supported by her husband, John Hignett. They appreciate only too well that the apparently idyllic setting has some major drawbacks. The steep hillside continually creeps down towards the river; the damp soil constantly erodes adjacent stonework, while penetrating east winds and harsh winter frosts cause severe damage to both the soft Westwood lime-stone and the plants. Each winter the statues are now clothed with aluminium foil wraps and Mediterranean plants such as *Phillyrea latifolia*, *Crataegus oxyacantha 'Gireoudii'* and bay also need winter protection.

The Hignetts' enthusiasm for a seemingly daunting task is boundless, but they have an equally enthusiastic head gardener, Rex Butler. Throughout the 1986 summer, the colonnade had to be anchored by guy ropes, and in the winter half of the supporting terrace wall was rebuilt. In 1987, a 3ft/1m gap was excavated behind the rear cloisters adjacent to the bank, allowing air to circulate freely and preventing the imminent collapse of the north side of the cloisters. John Hignett has designs for the completion of the unfinished Japanese garden by the diversion of spring waters from half a mile away and discrete illumination is being considered.

This view from an upper floor of the Manor shows part of the main garden and kitchen garden, which is entered through a door beneath the statue of the dying gladiator. At the far end, is a magnificent vista (see overleaf) created by Peto from an elevated mount down to the Manor. This winter picture exemplifies how an architectural garden retains its form, beauty and charm all year.

Left: Casement window. Overleaf: Elevated view over terraces towards the cloisters.   8 November 1986

COLOUR THEMES

THROUGHOUT the day subtle variations in garden colours take place. At high latitudes, as in Britain, the oblique light is softer than in subtropical and tropical climates. Pastel shades look best in the soft diffuse light produced by a thin cloud cover, while hot reds and oranges appear more striking in harsh, direct tropical sunlight. Water enriches the colour of stone or brick-work, and in dusty regions such as Xi'an in China, a shower of rain can revive a green landscape.

Our eye perceives colour before it appreciates shape. In photographs and paintings red demands our attention even if it is an indistinct impressionistic image. Individual clumps of red flowers and foliage planted in a red border, as at Hidcote Manor in Gloucestershire, will be distinguished more clearly if they are surrounded by green—their complementary colour. As an artist, Gertrude Jekyll appreciated more than many garden designers the importance of carefully controlled use of colour. She knew that blue flowers appear more intensely blue if interspersed with pale yellow blooms. A keen photographer herself, she recorded the summer borders in her Surrey garden at Munstead wood using autochrome—an early colour photographic process.

The introduction of colour into a garden must involve consideration not only of foliage or flower colour, but also for how long it will be lit by the sun and from which direction. For example, an evergreen hedge such as yew can appear almost black unless it is lit directly by the sun; whereas holly leaves appear lighter because they are shiny and reflect some light.

Permanent colour in a temperate garden is provided by evergreens and architectural features—red brick paths, walls and buildings, grey stone walls and statues. The expansive eighteenth-century landscape gardens are predominantly green, broken only by stonework or a sheet of silver or blue water. Few modern small gardens are restricted to a monochrome theme, the green garden in Savannah (p71) is a notable exception. Where single colour themes are used in part of a garden the result can be very effective (p68), unlike the linear gardens typical of suburbia, which present a confusing kaleidoscope of colours seen from a train window—a yellow *Forsythia* here, a flowering currant there—without any thought of the overall picture.

Gardens in rural settings often borrow the country-side view. Sutton Park (p26) and the Lutyens–Jekyll garden at Hestercombe (p30) have been planted so that the colours near the boundary lead the eye naturally to the fields, woods or hills beyond. In the Thameside garden (p103) the pink magnolia flowers are enhanced against the blue sky, while the dominant greens of the lawns and hedges in the sunken garden at Chenies Manor (p108) offset the hues of the herbaceous plants.

Yellow, gold, red, purple, silver or glaucous blue foliage provides a contrast to the usual green. Ornamental conifers retain their colour throughout the year, whereas deciduous trees and shrubs colour up for a limited, but much longer period than flowers. The rapid way colour emphasis can change in a herbaceous border is shown by the pair of pictures, taken a week apart, at Bramdean House (pp72 and 74)

Colour used sparingly, as in most oriental gardens can be highly effective. I can recall a striking arrangement of potted plants behind a raised pool in a courtyard of the Myriad Years Monastery on Emei Shan in Sechuan Province, China; all the plants were evergreen except for a pink flowered azalea which was perfectly reflected in the pool.

Authentic colour photography can convey the use of planned colour and associated colour planting in the garden much more successfully than any verbal or written description.

A Purple Parterre

A purple mail box indicates a note of non-conformity among the expansive houses nestling sedately between trees in a residential street of Atlanta, Georgia. On entering the recently-built house, you soon realize that Susan Hamilton has a passion for purple. Late in December, a huge Christmas tree festooned with purple baubles and bows greeted us inside the front door. Purple pervades every room, sometimes discretely as a radio in the kitchen, but also expansively as the entire decor of the dining room.

Purple has now invaded the garden too. In the front courtyard, Susan Hamilton wanted a low maintenance garden in a style contemporary with the modern house. So she commissioned Tim Rees, Director of the Inchbald School of Garden Design in London, to create one. Susan Hamilton, herself an artist, with a great interest in abstract paintings, was most enthusiastic about the parterre design. 'I saw it as an outdoor painting inspired by Miro's work.' Not surprisingly, it was she who opted for the purple expanses within the parterre. Tim Rees had been experimenting in his London garden with ways of making artificially coloured gravels and so he suggested spraying marble chippings with weather-resistant paint. No purple shades were available as small cans of hand sprays, but eventually iris, amethyst and deep purple car sprays were found. The next problem was that when the chips were sprayed *in situ* they tended to stick together, so they were painted individually and dried before being spread over the ground.

Atlanta is a city where the summer temperature can rise to 32°C, yet in winter it may drop to below freezing; such extremes severely limit the range of plants grown there. The courtyard area of the Hamilton's garden has a protected microclimate. In summer, the heat is kept down by increasing the humidity with regular irrigation; while in winter, the huge glass windows radiate enough heat to take the edge off the worst frosts. Over four hundred dwarf box, *Buxus sempervirens* 'Suffruticosa', were planted out in May 1985, and have survived into their third summer. They are clipped once a year in March. After two years, the colours of the chippings are as good as new. The purple shades are offset with larger areas of sombre grey chips surrounded by beige paths and cream walls. As Tim Rees points out, 'The advantage of using sprays is that the colours can, if necessary, be revitalized easily.' The concept of using coloured areas as a contrast to box designs is not new, for coloured earths were used in the seventeenth century *parterres de broderie*. Two centuries later, William Andrews Nesfield created parterres in a similar style, using coloured gravels. Sadly, the white and blue gravels were not replaced when his scroll and feather design was restored at Broughton Hall in Yorkshire at the turn of the century. With such a wide range of new materials and contemporary patterns providing inspiration, it is refreshing to see new thoughts being given to the use of parterres in garden design.

This view from a guest bedroom, showing the largest (32ft/9.7m × 11ft/3.3m) of three parterres, was taken after a morning of steady drizzle had thoroughly wetted the surface. Susan Hamilton was delighted that my visit had coincided with rain: 'When it rains, . . . it adds extra depth to all the colours which I can see all year round from every window in the front of the house.'

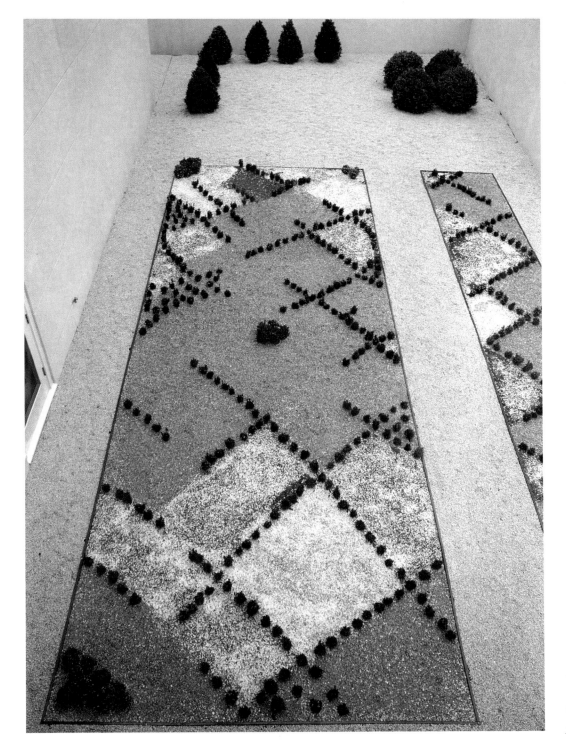

A parterre designed by
Tim Rees in Atlanta,
Georgia.
31 December 1985

Vibrant Colour

CRATHES CASTLE

Thrusting skywards, Crathes Castle is by any standards both impressive and romantic. Built of rough granite and covered with harling (Scottish roughcast) it is topped with small round bartizan towers bearing conical roofs. For more than three centuries, the Burnett family occupied Crathes—one of the best preserved sixteenth-century castles in Scotland.

The magnificent 12ft/4m-high yew hedges, bordering two sides of the croquet lawn, date back to 1702 when the garden was first laid out; but over two centuries had elapsed before the garden was skilfully remodelled by Sir James and Lady Sybil Burnett of Leys. At much the same time as Sir Harold Nicholson and Vita Sackville-West were creating their renowned garden at Sissinghurst in Kent, the Burnetts were developing their own garden rooms. Sir James' love of trees and shrubs perfectly complemented Lady Burnett's knowledge of herbaceous plants and her eye for colour.

During the period between the two World Wars, the Burnetts began to develop the gardens, each with its own distinct theme or colour scheme. They include four herbaceous borders—white, double, blue and June; the fountain or blue garden; the rose garden; the camel garden (with two raised beds in the centre) and the trough garden. The vista along the June borders looking towards the castle, is always a popular one for photographers. But the last garden to be made by Lady Burnett, the colour garden, is the most original with its bold colour associations. Completed in 1932, yellows, reds and bronzes are the predominant colours.

This view from the castle shows the centre of the colour garden with a square pool surrounded by four upright, immaculately shaped right-angle yew hedges. Their shapes are repeated in four beds outside, informally planted with bronze, red and yellow woody and herbaceous plants. By 1978, a major replanting was necessary to re-establish the original colour scheme. No plans existed of the garden, so when Eric Robson, Gardens Adviser to The National Trust for Scotland, advised on the replanting, he had to rely on the knowledge of the then head gardener, Douglas MacDonald. He also referred to his own photographs taken in 1960. As a result of the severe 1980 winter, summer drought in 1981 and smothering by perennial weeds, these beds were replanted again in spring 1985.

Inside the south-facing wall, original *Cotinus coggygria* 'Foliis purpureis' plants still exist underplanted with *Alchemilla mollis*. Additional red-leaved plants include *Vitis vinifera* 'Purpurea', *Corylus maxima* 'Atropurpurea' (this is cut down annually) and *Berberis thunbergii atropurpurea*; while *Senecio laxifolius*, *Rudbeckia newmanii* and *Solidago* 'Peter Pan' provide contrasting yellow flowers. Plants in the broad west-facing border include *Salvia fulgens*, rambler roses 'Veilchenblau' with crimson-purple flowers and 'Easlea's Golden Rambler' with rich yellow flowers, glossy green foliage and reddish thorns.

From the public rooms in the castle there are several elevated views of the other gardens, including tantalizing glimpses of the golden garden. This was developed from Gertrude Jekyll's ideas in her book *Colour Schemes for the Flower Garden*, but created in 1973 after Lady Burnett died. Striking though the various colour schemes are, sight should not be lost of some magnificent trees in this gem of a Deeside garden.

Right-angle beds and yew hedges round the central pool in the colour garden. 10 August 1986

Embellishing the Stonework

HADDON HALL

The walk up to Haddon Hall, perched 500ft/ 152m up on a Derbyshire limestone outcrop, gives no indication of the glorious gardens to come. The west front of this medieval stone house is bare and somewhat austere, but the turrets, watchtowers, castellations and battlemented walls cannot fail to intrigue. Inside the lower courtyard, are the first of many climbing roses and a recently replanted herb garden. Most of the gardens lie to the south of the house and in midsummer the first glimpse of them is quite breathtaking. Everywhere roses embellish the stonework; they festoon balustrades, clothe walls, and enliven beds.

To appreciate Haddon Hall garden today, a brief mention of the past history must be given. The Hall is listed in the 1087 Domesday Survey as being held by William Peveral, an illegitimate son of William the Conqueror. In 1170, it passed to the Vernon family, who owned it for four hundred years. The romantic setting at Haddon inspired the love story of Dorothy Vernon's escape one night from the Hall in the 1550s to elope with her lover, John Manners. She ran through the garden across the packhorse bridge over the River Wye (now known as Dorothy Vernon's bridge), where John Manners was waiting with horses. They certainly married in Leicestershire and inherited the Hall after Dorothy's father, Sir George Vernon, died in 1567. Sir John Manners transformed the Long Gallery into the magnificent room we see today, exceptionally well lit by the diamond panes in their curvaceous lead supports (p10) of the mullioned and transomed windows which line three sides of the room. The south-facing windows with those in the Great Chamber, afford splendid views on to the gardens; yet at the beginning of this century they were far from splendid. In 1703, when the Ninth Earl of Rutland was given the Dukedom of Rutland, the family moved to Belvoir Castle near Grantham in Lincolnshire leaving the Hall with all its furnishings untouched for two centuries. When the Ninth Duke returned in 1912 it was like stepping into a time capsule, and he devoted the rest of his life, over a quarter of a century, to restoring both the Hall and the gardens.

Huge trees were felled and the gardens cleared. The stone terraces, steps and balustrades were once again revealed; later to be embellished with trees, shrubs, perennials and roses within a formal framework. The series of terraces follow the contours of the hill towards the Wye. At right angles to the south front, is a fine seventeenth-century balustraded terrace pierced by steps down to a lawned terrace with a rectangular pool and fountain. This terrace is supported by huge retaining walls with outsized buttresses. Tom Pope, the head gardener, is now broadening the range of plants in the walls and buttresses to prolong the flowering season. If proof was needed that delphiniums thrive on being watered, 8ft/2.4m high spikes were produced beneath the Long Gallery as a result of the abnormally wet June in 1987. Above them, the pink flowers of the climbing rose 'Madame Grégoire Staechelin' adorn the walls.

When Haddon was originally built, little thought was given to creating gardens on a seemingly unpromising site, but the steep gradient admirably suited the construction of descending terraces. Even without living embellishments, the gardens are striking; with them, they are a glorious celebration of a romantic creation.

Climbing roses adorn curved leaded lights and stonework of the Long Gallery. 3 July 1987

A White Garden

BARRINGTON COURT

hen The National Trust acquired Barrington Court in Somerset in 1907, it was very dilapidated and the garden non-existent; but in 1920 it was let to Colonel A A Lyle on a full repairing lease. Financed by the family's sugar company, he restored the Tudor house, converted the seventeenth-century stable block into a house and approved plans for the gardens, which he sadly did not live to see.

Forbes and Tate, architects for the house, also drew up elaborate plans for developing some ten acres of garden. Gertrude Jekyll designed planting plans based on their design, but only a few were implemented. The old farmyard adjacent to the stable block was transformed into three symmetrically designed gardens with distinct colour schemes. The warm colours in the Lily Garden are in sympathy with, although not identical to, Gertrude Jekyll's plans. Azaleas and *Hemerocallis dumortieri* are planted in raised beds in specially imported lime-free soil. Both winter and summer bedding plants are used to extend the flowering season of the shrubs and perennials.

The adjacent White Garden, the inspiration of Christine Middleton, was originally a rose garden filled with hybrid tea and floribunda roses. The white garden was planted in 1986 with a selection of silver and white annuals and herbaceous plants; *Viola* 'Sissinghurst' and *Aconitum* × *bicolor* 'Ivorine' being among the first white flowers to open.

The most famous white garden in England is, of course, Vita Sackville-West's creation at Sissinghurst Castle in Kent, best seen from a window in the tower. Here, the impact of the white flowers and grey foliage is greatly enhanced by the green box-edged beds and green foliage. At Barrington, green turf surrounding the eight beds arranged in a circle around a statue, produces the same effect. In August 1987 these beds were packed with *Nicotiana* 'Domino white' and 'Lime green', *Petunia* 'White joy', *Matricaria* 'White gem' and white *Allysum*. In each corner of this walled garden is a large triangular bed with *Crambe cordifolia*, *Galtonia candicans*, *Lysimachia barystachys*, *Artemisia* 'Powis Castle' and *A. absinthium* 'Lambrook silver', *Oenothera* 'Wedding Bells', white sweet peas and many other plants.

Light stonework, white and cream flowers, as well as grey foliage, reflects so much light on a bright sunny day that the subtle shades, as well as the surface textures, are indiscernible. They are best seen (and photographed) in a soft diffuse light produced by a thin cloud cover. A white garden or border, takes on a special magic of its own when viewed by the light of a full moon.

The east wall of the White Garden is decorated with a row of oval windows with leaded lights. It is worth visiting the lavatories if only to glimpse the White Garden through one of these attractive windows. A portion of the Iris Garden is seen here beyond the west wall where the colour theme encompasses pinks, mauves and blues, starting with *Iris germanica* followed by lavenders, petunias, clematis, heliotropes, *Salvia hormonium* and *S. farinacea*.

The present policy at Barrington is not to rigorously reproduce an identical planting year after year, rather to maintain the particular colour schemes with slight variations to the theme so that it gradually evolves from one year to another.

Green turf sets off a selection of annuals and perennials in the White Garden. 5 August 1987

A Green Garden

SAVANNAH GARDEN, GEORGIA

Spring comes early to the south-eastern seaboard of the United States. In south-east Georgia lies Savannah, founded in 1732, the last of England's thirteen colonies in America. At the end of March, the first azaleas begin to flower and soon afterwards every street is enlivened with azaleas and dogwoods in full bloom.

Recently, many private Savannah gardens invariably hidden behind walls, have been transformed by creating designs with year-round interest in the smallest of backyards. However, it is not vibrant azaleas which draw the eye to focus beyond the window in the gate of 222 East Jones Street, but the attractive Victorian fountain in the centre of the parterre. James Morton, who admits to being a frustrated sculptor, has clearly relished the several years spent transforming his yard into a harmonious entity. Colour has been used in a subtle way in this essentially green garden.

When he bought the house in 1973 all he found was a flat L-shaped dirt yard with a 90ft/30m long strip running back from the road and a 60ft/20m strip running at right angles behind the house. The only original plants are a pair of cherry laurel *Prunus caroliniana* trees arching over the cast iron 1870 fountain, the focal point of the sunken garden. This part was created by digging out the soil and throwing it up at the sides to make the raised borders. Frequently smaller elements of the overall design change; the area around the fountain was at one time grass, now it is a parterre of Japanese box, *Buxus mircophylla*. This species was chosen because European box *Buxus sempervirens* will not survive the sultry Savannah summers. A mulch of *Pinus australis* needles gives springy paths with a uniform colour.

James was inspired by '. . . ideas drawn from gardens seen in England, France and Italy which I scaled down. My dedication to the task was spurred on by the inspirational interest of my friend and octogenarian gardener, Louisa Farrand Wood, who has kindled a renascence of gardening pleasure in her adopted Savannah. It is not surprising that she is the niece of Beatrix Farrand, America's equivalent to England's Gertrude Jekyll. Louisa's keen sense of design made me modify a circular topiary *Ilex vomitoria* into a compass garden simply by clipping the top into the initial letters of the four compass points. This garden now functions as a pivot point for the two main axes of the garden.' Plants in the raised borders include clump bamboo, *Fatsia*, palmetto palms, Savannah holly and ferns which together create a tropical lushness in contrast to the formal court. Along one edge a many-bordered carpet effect is achieved. Behind the outer brick edging are strips of ivy, dwarf *Liriope* and carpet bugle *Ajuga reptans*.

Throughout the garden James Morton uses symmetrical pairs of plants, urns and potted plants to define and emphasize entrances to compartments. A closer look at this delightful garden reveals many subtle touches. For example, the filigree curtains of Spanish moss *Tillandsia usneoides* (not a true moss, but an epiphytic bromeliad) hang from a pair of crape myrtle *Lagerstroemia indica* trees behind the fountain. Creeping fig *Ficus pumila* is allowed to grow on the west wall of the house up to the height of the boundary wall, so that the line is continued round the garden. The happy marriage of shrubs and potted plants with ornaments makes it a garden full of interest in any season.

Victorian fountain in the sunken court viewed through the gate. 14 April 1987

A Floral Tapestry

BRAMDEAN HOUSE

*L*it by the early evening light, the double herbaceous borders at Bramdean House, in Hampshire, are the quintessence of the English midsummer. These views from the upper floor of the house, emphasize the full extent of the borders as well as highlighting the individual plants judiciously chosen and planted to create a perfect colour tapestry. They also graphically illustrate how the colour emphasis in a herbaceous border can change within a week. In early summer, blue predominates with *Nepeta* 'Six Hills Giant', Pacific hybrid delphiniums and giant comfrey *Symphytum uplandicum* intermingled with harmonious white clumps of *Crambe cordifolia*, before the yellow phase begins to take over with *Inula magnifica, Thalictrum speciosissimum* and *Aruncus dioicus* predominating.

There has been a garden at Bramdean for over two centuries and the location of the borders dates back to the 1850s, although the herbaceous borders were only created by the late Mrs Cecil Feilden shortly after the Second World War. Her daughter, Mrs Hady Wakefield, not only inherited the garden but also her mother's enthusiasm for it. In the autumn of 1984 she decided to revamp the entire 112ft/34m long borders by replanting the informal plants in a formal way, making one side the mirror image of the other, thereby intensifying the overall picture.

In most gardens, borders are invariably created in front of walls or hedges, so they are protected from the elements on one side at least. At Bramdean, however, they are surrounded by lawns, so they can be viewed from any direction. As Mrs Wakefield points out: 'This makes for much more careful planting; the height, shape, colour and texture have to be considered from all four sides. My aim is to plant in such a way that it is possible to look through plants at others behind, instead of producing a solid wall. It is very important to have pointed spikes as well as rounded shapes.'

Tall herbaceous plants are always prone to wind damage and the open standing borders at Bramdean offer no protection. The plants are cleverly supported by a combination of pea sticks and semicircular iron supports 2, 4 or 6ft/0.6 1.2 or 1.8m high respectively, in such a way that they are virtually invisible when the borders are in full bloom. Hazel twigs are ingeniously made into bird cage supports for training species sweet peas, while miniature wooden hurdles only 20in/50cm high, from chestnut coppices in Kent, prevent the marginal *Nepeta* clumps from flopping on to the central grass path.

Long before the borders reach their peak of perfection in July, Mrs Wakefield looks forward to the first signs of life emerging through the ground after the long winter dormancy. She can then check the delphiniums have not been devoured by slugs and anticipate the summer glory in the months ahead. The first colour is provided in May by bulbs and euphorbias; while after the mid-summer flowers have faded Michaelmas daisies and nerines come into their own. Great care has been taken to ensure the flower colours do not compete with the brick walled kitchen garden beyond the borders. From the house the eye is automatically led up the garden's main axis, from the herbaceous walk through the gateway and the grass path in the kitchen garden to the gazebo, complete with cupola, some 325ft/100m due north.

OPPOSITE: *Ascending double herbaceous borders. 2 July 1986* OVERLEAF: *Borders 8 July 1986*

FRAMING THE VIEW

WHEN house and gardens are designed together as a unit, windows invariably frame a specific feature; but even when the garden is developed at a later stage, existing windows can be used to frame garden pictures. Throughout this book there are references to people who have created their garden, or an aspect of it, specifically to be viewed from a particular window in the house.

The cloistered courtyards so popular in Moorish and Spanish gardens, provide changing frames for the inner courtyard scene. The widespread use of ornate apertures in the walls of oriental gardens is discussed in Chapter 8. In western gardens, apertures as features tend to be much less common, although the *clair-voie* or *clair-voyée*, originating from French and Dutch gardens, was introduced to Britain during the seventeenth century. This opening in a wall or above a gate at the end of an allée or path, allowed glimpses of the distant view. Apertures in walls and hedges help to break up a solid expanse of brick, stone or foliage; they also serve to frame intimate views within, or to provide tantalizing glimpses of broader vistas outside. They automatically entice the eye to focus beyond the screen.

Twelve oval peep-holes are a notable feature in the outer stone wall of the oval garden at Heywood in Ireland (p85); while two small peep-holes pierce a brick wall at Polesden Lacey in Surrey giving framed views in both directions. An aperture in the top of a high gate, or between a stone or brick arch over the gate, also makes a peep-hole. At Biltmore in North Carolina, trelliswork bordering a covered walkway in the Walled Garden is pierced by repeated oval and round-headed apertures. Windows in grottoes made of roughly hewn rocks, as at Stourhead in Wiltshire and in the Japanese garden cave at Tully (p122) have an irregular outline to their frame.

Two variations on a theme for larger wall-openings, softened with plants, are illustrated in Jekyll and Weaver's *Gardens for Small Country Homes*. In both, plants hang down from an overhead beam supported on vertical piers and one wall has plants cascading from a window box. The Australian architect, Raymond McGrath, incorporated outsized picture frames into balconies on top of a Surrey house in Chertsey so they framed the ancient cedar trees in the eighteenth-century parkland.

Ruined buildings with windows at normal viewing height can make a striking framework to a garden (p82); but elevated frames, like the huge gothic window in the Priory Church at Newstead Abbey in Nottinghamshire, always look on to the sky. However, at Heywood, a fifteenth-century tracery window was incorporated into a romantic ruin with a high viewpoint, specifically to frame the picturesque landscape, complete with lake, below.

Apertures in living walls have to be regularly clipped to retain clean edges; but their shape and position can, if necessary, be modified to suit a changing view. A line of semicircular windows in a solid hedge is illustrated in Thomas H Mawson's book *The Art and Craft of Garden Making*; while narrower, deeper openings pierced the serpentine tunnel in the elaborate Bower Garden at Elvaston (p91). Pleached hedges bordering a boundary; the walls of a tunnel or an allée, may be suitable for introducing windows; for example, at Horsted Place in Sussex there are several fine views across the South Downs through rectangular windows in pleached limes. Windows are usually cut at right angles to a hedge, but a private French garden outside Paris has elongated windows cut at oblique angles in a large hornbeam hedge, so that each one frames a different view.

A Forgotten Masterpiece

HAWKSTONE PARK

In its heyday—from the mid-eighteenth century to the early part of this century—Hawkstone Park in Shropshire was a tourist attraction of national repute. The Hawkstone Hotel was built in 1790 specifically to cater for tourists who took several days to explore the exhilarating walks. Now, apart from local people, few know the Park exists; the main attraction is a golf course laid out on the plains in 1935.

Hawkstone Hall was purchased by Sir Rowland Hill in 1556 but it was not until the eighteenth century that his descendant, and namesake the First Baronet, extended the Park to encompass a naturally picturesque landscape of wooded hills. This he further embellished with follies, and a grotto. His son, Sir Richard Hill, added the 2½ mile long stretch of water known as Hawk Lake. He also carved catwalks from solid rock and built a Swiss log-and-rope bridge across a chasm to add to the excitement of the ornamental walks.

By the time Dr Johnson visited Hawkstone in July 1774, the grotto was complete. The scenery at Hawkstone clearly made a lasting impression on him: 'He that mounts the precipices at Hawkstone wonders how he came hither, and doubts how he shall return. His walk is an adventure, and his departure an escape.' None of the sandstone cliffs are much more than 500ft/150m high, but their precipitous sides rise steeply from the north Shropshire plain, so that anyone who suffers from vertigo may still find the breathtaking view from Grotto Hill quite daunting. On fine days it is possible to see the Horseshoe Pass at Llangollen.

Over the years, *Rhododendron ponticum* scrub has invaded paths and even though some have recently been cleared, it is inadvisable to venture on to the Hawkstone cliffs without a guide. Mr Jack Jones, a sprightly octogenarian, is proud to be the fourth generation of Hawkstone guides from his family. His 2½ hour tour takes in all the main landmarks and follies. He will lead you along the 300 ft/91m long dark passage into the labyrinth of man-made tunnels, reputed by some to be old copper mines, for there are mines on the opposite hill. Jack Jones has his own theory; he believes it could have been a fortress. The elevated situation is perfect, aided by the fact the plain below was at one time a swamp. Roof apertures, which now provide a welcome glimmer of light in the dark grotto, more than likely let out smoke from fires inside. Towards the end of the underground tour, the rooms are lit by shafts of light from windows, roughly hewn in rock, looking out on to the cliffs beyond. Until 1940, the walls of the last room were encrusted with shells and stalactites, while the porthole windows were decorated with stained glass, but they were all vandalized during the war years. Some of the follies have also been vandalized or destroyed by weathering, but the Obelisk, the White Tower and the Red Castle, have been listed as being of historic interest.

In 1987, the results of a feasibility study sponsored by the Countryside Commission, English Heritage and Shropshire County Council for the restoration and management of this unique and historic park were published. Plans have been agreed with local authorities and landowners, and a Hawkstone Trust is to be set up to raise funds over a ten-year period; so that once again the Park will be open on a regular basis to delight and enthrall visitors.

An aperture in the grotto frames a knarled pine on Grotto Hill. 2 August 1986 or 7 May 1987

An Unimpeded View

RODMARTON MANOR

It comes as no surprise to learn that the garden at Rodmarton Manor in Gloucestershire was laid out at the same time as the Cotswold stone house, for each complements the other so well. In the early part of this century The Hon Claud and Mrs Biddulph wanted a family home with a notable garden. Eager to involve as many local craftsmen as possible, they commissioned Ernest Barnsley to design the gabled manor house which was built entirely from local stone and wood.

Barnsley also designed the basic framework of the garden, influenced no doubt, by his association with Reginald Blomfield, who was a strong advocate of a formal approach to gardening. William Scrubey was appointed head gardener; he proved to be a true garden craftsman who nurtured the garden for almost half a century. Scrubey was a short man and when Major and Mrs Anthony Biddulph inherited Rodmarton in 1954, they found all the limes around the forecourt and behind the house, had all been pleached to his height!

Rodmarton, like so many British gardens, was neglected during the war years, when pheasants took to nesting in the borders. Mrs Biddulph, assisted by two gardeners, gradually tamed the wilderness and began to introduce several features of her own. Reminiscent of Hidcote Manor and Crathes Castle (p64), yew hedges surround the series of inter-connecting gardens. There are also some splendid vistas, notably from the house looking out over a ha-ha.

The vista shown here, framed by a balcony in the house, overlooks a cluster of pleached limes to the 'Troughery'—a small topiary garden decorated with many stone troughs collected from the farm. Raised up on saddlestone supports, the troughs contain small plants which could easily become swamped by more robust ones in larger beds. Beyond the ordered garden, across the ha-ha, lies a natural floriferous meadow, with fluffy white umbels of Queen Anne's lace *Antheriscus sylvestris* beyond. In a small courtyard beneath the limes is a winter garden where plants such as crocus, hepaticas and several varieties of hellebores enliven the dullest of winter days. Snowdrops are also grown here, and all over the garden, for Mrs Biddulph has a passion for *Galanthus* species and varieties.

In the leisure garden, the first enclosures to be laid out by Mrs Biddulph, are floribunda and hybrid tea rose beds set in stone paving. Each bed is bordered with a different kind of ground cover plant to deter birds from pulling manure out on to the stonework. She also made the formal flagged terrace behind the house; divided into sections by yew hedges and decorated with topiary shapes, including peacocks, it exemplifies Blomfield's axiomatic belief that formal shape is an essential element in garden design.

A notable feature, dating back to the time when the garden was first laid out, is the magnificent Long Garden with Ernest Barnsley's summerhouse as its focal point. Showy double borders planted with a mixture of roses and perennials are interrupted by a small circular pool with four stone seats each surrounded by a high-backed yew hedge in the style of a settle.

Mrs Biddulph's interest in gardens was initiated by a childhood love of wild flowers; now she is contemplating creating a species rose garden, to further embellish her garden with its strong architectural framework.

The view across the trough garden looks out to the fields beyond. 29 May 1987

Framework to a Picture

The gothic-style frames to the windows looking on to an old Berkshire kitchen garden date back to 1955 when Russell Page designed the garden. In his book, *The Education of a Gardener*, Page has a black and white photograph showing the formal box-edged flower garden with square beds subdivided by internal box divisions. The small beds were designed for planting with spring and summer bedding.

This garden was commissioned by Mrs Reginald (Daisy) Fellowes after her husband died. She lived at Donnington Grove, a splendid example of Strawberry Hill Gothick architecture, but she wanted a place of her own to escape from the house guests. For her retreat she chose a small building on the estate, overlooking a walled garden, to be converted into an eighteenth-century cottage orné in the style of the main house.

When the present owners, Mr and Mrs Guy Elmes, moved there in 1980, the garden had deteriorated owing to the cottage being let to a series of tenants, one of whom destroyed all the box infilling by spraying the beds with weed killer. The low bedding plants had been replaced by taller perennials and shrubs which tended to obscure the box edging. Mrs Elmes has retained some of the plants she inherited in the four square-edged box beds, including paeonies and a *Ceanothus*; she has also added Iceberg roses. Two of the beds, she has filled with herbs. Throughout the garden, her enthusiasm for *Clematis* is evident, with several plants intertwining through rambler roses on a series of iron arches running along the east side of the garden.

The severe 1980–81 winter killed a large *Clematis montana* growing over a small summer house backing on to the outer wall. Flowers of new clematis plants put in at the four corners of the summer house now cover the thick thatch formed from the old dead stems. The path on the right of the box-edged beds originally led through an opening in the end wall. This has now been filled by an impressively solid door from Newbury jail, unfortunately masked in this view by a large lilac. Another exit from the garden leads via a pear tunnel into the old kitchen garden where a children's yew maze is still maintained.

In his book Russell Page argues that where space is restricted, a formal design works well. 'I like to keep the pattern of a formal garden very simple and to use squares, circles and rectangles outlined by narrow paved paths and edge them, as often as not, with lavender, box, rosemary or santolina. I see them as gardens compartmented like a Persian rug, a series of simple shapes to fill with flowers in any one of a hundred different ways.' From early on, Page developed a passion for plants. His awareness of plant form lead him to describe himself as a landscape *gardener* rather than a landscape architect.

Several gardens featured in this book show how box edges bring a sense of order to any garden (pp36, 71, 92, 95, 96, 98–9 and 137). The colours and height of the infill can be varied over the years to suit the individual taste of different owners or, as Russell Page often visualized, with the changing season. He points out that we appreciate a garden by viewing it as a series of pictures from fixed points; in other words as if a sequence of stills frozen from a film or video.

The first picture we see each day is invariably framed by a window as we draw back the curtains.

Gothic-style windows look on to box-edged beds in an old kitchen garden. 16 June 1987

A Majestic Ruin

SUDELEY CASTLE

Nothing remains today of the Manor House at Sudeley in Gloucestershire, listed in the Domesday Book as an estate with a royal deer park. In the fifteenth century, the newly created Baron Sudeley, built a magnificent castle from the spoils of the French Wars; but after the defeat of the Lancastrian house during the Wars of the Roses, the Yorkist Edward IV succeeded to the throne and the Baron had to sell his castle to the king. Throughout Henry VIII's reign, Sudeley remained a Royal estate, but following his death, it was given to Sir Thomas Seymour, the brother of Henry's third wife, Jane Seymour. After Thomas Seymour was appointed Lord Sudeley, he married Katherine Parr, Henry's sixth wife, who died from puerperal fever a few days after giving birth to her daughter, Mary.

The castle was attacked during the Civil War, and in 1648 the victorious Parliamentarians ordered the destruction of Sudeley. All that remained of the magnificent Banqueting Hall were a few windows and fireplaces—virtually the same as today. The fifteenth-century tithe barn was probably gutted by fire at this time.

For nearly two centuries the ruins remained untouched, until parts of Sudeley Castle were restored by bachelor brothers, John and William Dent, between 1830-7. The medieval Banqueting Hall was imaginatively left as a picturesque ruin. After their nephew, John Croucher Dent inherited, his wife Emma Brocklehurst devoted her life to restoring the castle and the grounds. On the east side of the castle lay a large rectangular area with a square sunken garden filling the southern part outside the Banqueting Hall. When the Dents began work on the sunken garden in 1850, they found a fountain pool, the centrepiece of the old elaborate parterre, almost certainly laid out in Katherine Parr's time. Topiary featured strongly in the restoration of what is now known as the Queen's Garden. A parterre was surrounded by immaculately clipped squares of box. The north and south sides of the garden were flanked by huge double yew hedges, still present today. Resembling fortifications, each has a central path providing a cool walk in hot weather with arches and round peep-holes offering views on to the inner garden. Outside the southern edge and along the entire eastern side of the ractangular area is a raised terrace walk and stone balustrade. Raised walks were popular in Tudor times, used as a substitute for a mount to give an elevated view of the garden. At Sudeley, they still offer fine views of the parterre, the adjacent park and the Cotswold hills beyond. To the north of the Queen's Garden lies St Mary's church where Katherine Parr is buried.

The ground floor windows of the ruined Banqueting Hall, mellowed by centuries of weathering, frame views on to the Queen's Garden in one direction and on to the inner courtyard in the other. In between the flagstones laid beside the wall facing on to the courtyard, a few perennials and shrubs provide contrasting colour to the stonework. Windows in the shell of the wisteria-clad tithe barn also serve as frames to garden pictures across the ornamental pond.

The huge upper mullioned windows of the ruined Banqueting Hall are so well preserved, it is possible to visualize the magnificent setting overlooking the parterre, used to lavishly entertain eminent visitors, including Elizabeth I, all those centuries ago.

A window in the ruined Banqueting Hall frames the view on to the Queen's Garden. 3 June 1987

An Irish Cameo

HEYWOOD GARDEN

The garden of Heywood, in the Salesian College near Ballinakill, has two distinct parts. There is the eighteenth-century landscape park created by the Reverend Frederick Trench planting many trees, and later embellished by the gothic gatehouse and romantic ruin, (complete with a fifteenth-century stone tracery window from the Friary at Aghaboe) erected by his son Michael. The second part was not begun until 1906, when Colonel Hutcheson Poë commissioned Edwin Lutyens to design a formal garden adjacent to the house which already enjoyed a superb outlook across fields dotted with trees to distant hills. In 1941, the house and estate were bought by the Salesian Fathers for their Missionary College. After an accidental fire destroyed the house in 1950, a new school was built a short distance away, but the garden remained intact.

Running the entire length of the old house, Lutyens built a flagstone terrace looking out over a broad lawn terrace supported by a huge buttressed wall, to the vista beyond. On the west side of the lawn is a magnificent pergola with a rectangular window overlooking the fields and lake below. The east end of the terrace leads via a pleached lime alley to a walled oval garden. Sandstone from local quarries was used for the high wall and the paving, as well as the raised beds in this highly architectural garden. Twelve oval peep-holes pierce the outer wall, allowing ever-changing scenes of the distant hills to be glimpsed.

This picture is a cameo seen from outside the wall looking into the Oval Garden. Although not as Lutyens intended, it does show some of the features within, notably part of the oval stone-terraced borders with a central pool set into lawn. Not visible is the pavilion positioned opposite the pleached lime alley, no doubt to provide a view across the pool to the alley; however the view is obscured by a huge stone fountain, which seems to be out of proportion with the pool. Colonel Hutcheson Poë may have commissioned the fountain in Paris in 1911, for Lutyens disapproved of this outsized addition to his design. Eight brass turtles, each resting on a stone mound positioned equidistantly around the water's edge, used to play water into the pool. To complement the curving wall and terraces, Lutyens used straight flights of shallow steps; whereas curving steps descend into the square Great Plat at Hestercombe (p30).

The garden at Heywood is now planted with roses, perennials and some annuals; not at all as originally planned by Gertrude Jekyll in 1910. Sadly, her plans cannot be traced, but photographs taken in 1918 for *Country Life* provide records of the garden shortly after it was completed in 1912. The pool is shown as a clear expanse of water filled to the rim, so it reflects its surroundings to their best advantage.

It is remarkable that the garden is now maintained single-handed by Father Brewster, an important factor which Graham Stuart Thomas had to bear in mind when he prepared his recent planting scheme. Already the architectural features of this important Lutyens garden have been restored, the stonework has been repointed, the pavilion re-roofed and the pergola timbers renewed. With the active support of the Irish Garden Plant Society, the planting will soon be restored, so the harmonious blending of plants and stone within a formal design can, like Hestercombe, be enjoyed once more.

The Oval Garden glimpsed through a peep-hole window. 19 August 1987

Borrowed Vistas

PENSHURST PLACE

*A*pproaching Penshurst village along a winding country road near Tonbridge in Kent, past green fields and chestnut coppices, there is a magnificent view of the manor house set back from the parkland. Records of the first owner of Penshurst Place go back to the thirteenth century, but a house was recorded on this site in the Domesday Book (1085). The house as it stands includes the finest and most complete fourteenth-century manor house in England. Late in the eighteenth century, a visitor described Penshurst as a 'near romantic ruin', which may well explain why the garden was ignored by both Brown and Repton. From about 1818 a long chapter of restoration began and has continued. The terraces and walls are Tudor, but separating the garden into many compartments enclosed by high yew hedges, was the inspiration of the second Lord De L'Isle at the end of the last century.

From the State Dining Room there is a spectacular view looking on to the formal parterre known as the Italian Garden. In spring, the box-edged beds are filled with single yellow tulips, while pink 'Elizabeth Arden' roses provide summer colour. Until 1939, bedding plants were traditionally used in this garden, however when the present Lord De L'Isle inherited Penshurst after the Second World War, the gardens were neglected from lack of labour; so this large area was replanted specifically for easy maintenance.

Tucked away in one corner of the garden, at the end of a raised grass terrace walk on the west side of the parterre, are two openings in a boundary brick wall. One window, looking southwards, offers a spectacular view of the upper Medway valley and the Kent countryside in complete contrast to the adjacent formal Italian garden. In the distance is a pillbox, one of many built along the Medway for defending the south coast during the Second World War. The inside wall is in shadow for most of the day, but when the deciduous trees outside leaf out in early spring, the bright greens are accentuated by the unlit surrounding wall. Honeysuckle leaves festooning the wall echo the green vista; while beneath the window, encrusting orange lichens are a sure sign the air is free from atmospheric pollution. The view through the other window looking westwards towards the village has been blocked by a later building.

Another example of a borrowed vista can be seen at Penshurst via a window in a yew hedge bordering the main walk through the double herbaceous borders. Beyond the Middle Walk towering above the boundary wall, is the four-pinnacled tower of the parish church of St John the Baptist, with one of a pair of large tulip trees *Liriodendron tulipifera* flanking the Tudor doorway giving access from the garden to the church-yard.

For most visitors the main attraction of Penshurst is the unique house, but the obligatory walk through the gardens cannot fail to impress. Whatever the season, the varied enclosures offer delightful surprises, but a spring visit is an experience not to be missed. There are tulips in both the Spring and Italian gardens; drifts of bluebells enliven the grassy swards beneath the Kentish cobs in the Nut Garden and scent from the blossom on the avenues of old apple trees pervades the air. Penshurst has long been famous for its fruit trees; John Evelyn notes in his diary of July 1652: 'We went to see Penshurst famous for its gardens and excellent fruit.'

OPPOSITE: *Window in yew hedge frames Middle Walk. 24 May 1986*   OVERLEAF: *Boundary wall aperture. 15 May 1986*

87

FORMALITY

IN Tudor times, garden design became much more intricate as the passion for pattern in the form of mazes and knots developed. No sixteenth-century pleasure garden was complete without a knot garden—a geometrically symmetrical interlaced pattern made from low-growing or clipped evergreen plants. During this era, perhaps more than any other, the view from the window was enriched by the knot laid out beneath it. True knots were made by planting herbs so that the different coloured foliage interlaced, in some cases resembling a rope. The more complex knot gardens emulated embroidery; hence the references to garden knots being embroidered with herbs. Knot designs were inspired by contemporary embroidery, marquetry and plasterwork; indeed, it was not unknown for a person to produce designs for decorating both house and garden.

Early knots were laid out with interlaced rosemary, thyme and hyssop, with the spaces between either left bare or covered with coloured sand, gravel, fragmented bricks or tiles, even coal dust was used as a contrast to the living foliage. Later knots were infilled with flowers of one colour or, as more plants were introduced to Britain, with a variety of plants (p95). Summer knots made from summer savory, hyssop and wild strawberry were more ephemeral than herb knots, having to be sown or planted each year. In the seventeenth century, dwarf box knots became fashionable, maintaining their shape and colour all the year.

The parterre was an important focal point of French formal gardens. Unlike knots, of which many different designs could be seen in a garden, the typical parterre was laid out so that the two sides were mirror images with flowing curvaceous lines. Like knots, parterres were laid out adjacent to the house so the complete design could be seen stretched out as a living carpet beneath an upper window.

Most of the grand parterres laid out in Britain were cleared away when expansive landscaped gardens became fashionable in the eighteenth century. After prolonged summer drought the design of many of these 'lost' parterres, long since grassed over without trace from the ground, became visible from the air. An aerial photograph taken of Clumber Park in Nottinghamshire in 1949, revealed the Great Parterre laid out in the 1830s. Also in this year, the pattern of the paths of the Great Parterre (1694) at Chatsworth could be seen from the upper floor windows of the house. During the 1976 summer drought, an air balloon was used to photograph the remnants of the 'lost' parterres at Stowe.

Vegetable gardens can also be laid out in a formal way. The finest example of a *jardin potager* on a large scale can be seen at the Château de Villandry. Inspired by sixteenth-century engravings of Du Cerceau, the two-acre potager was constructed early this century as nine large squares, each containing many geometrically shaped beds planted with colourful vegetables and flowers to produce a living painting. The kitchen garden was originally laid out adjacent to the castle for the very practical reason that the seigneur needed to keep a watchful eye from the chateau windows over the recently imported vegetables from America and other parts of Europe.

No formal garden is complete without topiary forms and copious boxwood shapes, such as those in the *jardin d'ornament* at Villandry, designed by the Spanish artist Lozano. Two gardens with notable topiary features are included with architectural gardens on pp49 and 57. The formal gardens in this section range from a small scale knot garden to an exceptionally large parterre.

A Two-Toned Parterre

ELVASTON CASTLE COUNTRY PARK

The way a garden designer first sees the topography of a garden inevitably influences how he visualizes, and creates, the particular style. If 'Capability' Brown had seen the potential to create such a picturesque landscape at Elvaston Castle in Derbyshire, it is doubtful he would have turned down the commission by the third Earl of Harrington. Brown declined to lay out the grounds 'because the place is so flat, and there is such a want of capability about it'. He did present the Earl with six Cedars of Lebanon, five of which remain today.

Some years later, in 1830, the fourth Earl made William Barron, then only thirty years old, head gardener at Elvaston. Barron took up the challenge and created a unique and impressive garden. He began by planting elaborate multi-rowed avenues of conifers including Chilean pines, Japanese cedars, pines, cedars, firs and spruces. He soon perfected a technique for transplanting large trees over considerable distances, which enabled him to plant a notable garden within a decade. A large lake was also made together with several artificial rock works, including two circular moon gates overlooking the lake.

Facing the south front of the castle, Barron created an elaborate topiary garden, based on a seventeenth-century design by Daniel Marot, illustrated in *A Manual of the Coniferae* by Veitch in 1881. Known as the Bower Garden or *Mon Plaisir*, the main feature was a labyrinthine tunnel, made of arbor-vitae, *Thuja plicata*, pierced at intervals by small viewing windows. In the centre of the garden eight yew bowers provided shelter for seats facing on to a star-shaped bed. Chile pines or monkey puzzle trees, *Araucaria araucana* (*A. imbricata*) were liberally scattered throughout the Bower Garden. This South American conifer was first introduced to Britain in 1795 and was immensely popular in Victorian times.

Sadly, few people saw Elvaston garden in its heyday, for the fourth Earl was a recluse. Barron had strict instructions to exclude all visitors—with the exception of Queen Victoria! After the Earl died in 1851, the gardens were opened to the public at (the then) exhorbitant fee of three shillings, but escalating costs meant the original ninety gardeners had to be reduced tenfold, so trees were not vigorously thinned, although the garden was maintained well into this century. Indeed, an aerial photograph taken in 1954 shows an intact Bower Garden, although by no means so crisply defined as a century earlier. By the time the castle and garden were bought by Derbyshire County Council in 1968, the garden had suffered considerable neglect. An extensive programme of tree surgery was undertaken; but the collapsed Bower Garden was past restoration, so all the conifers were removed, apart from a topiary crown of green yew, some ball-shaped golden yews and some magnificent specimens of *Taxus baccata* 'Aurea' with branches thrusting skywards like an exploding firework. The Parks Department substituted the three-dimensional design in yew with an essentially two-dimensional design in green and golden box, by creating an imaginative two-toned Parterre Garden in 1970.

Visitors to Elvaston Castle Country Park can now enjoy both the spacious gardens and the wildlife. Unlike gardens which rely on seasonal colour for their interest, the fine trees, topiary and parterre gardens ensure Elvaston can be appreciated all year round.

Green and golden box Parterre Garden seen from upper floor of the castle. 18 June 1987

Ladies Garden with fleur-de-lys beds viewed from a window in the Council Chamber. 31 July 1987

Regal Symbols

BROUGHTON CASTLE

A moated island is the idyllic setting of Broughton Castle. This early fourteenth-century Oxfordshire manor house, later enlarged and embellished with castellated gatehouses and a curtain wall, was neglected early in the nineteenth century when the family moved to Kent. In 1837 virtually all the contents, including the swans on the moat, were sold in an eight-day sale. Diminishing family fortunes ensured that it was spared architectural 'improvements' during Victorian times, when invading ivy softened the stark walls.

From 1887–1910, the castle was let to the Lord and Lady Algernon Gordon-Lennox. Although rough pasture covered the entire island, Lady Algernon recognized its potential and rapidly transformed the site. In 1898 an account in *Country Life* extolled, 'Never in its history of nearly six centuries has Broughton presented such a fair spectacle.' Fortunately, the highly original gardens Lady Algernon created are well documented by contemporary photographs. The drawing room windows looked out on to yews clipped into dark green spirals with formal beds beyond. South of the castle she laid out the Ladies Garden on the site of the Elizabethan kitchens. This walled garden still retains its formal centre-piece of four box-hedged fleur-de-lys beds and two circular beds. The moat was transformed from a rank and stagnant ditch into a beautiful water garden with banks of native poppies and foxgloves.

By 1968, when the present Lord Saye and Sele inherited Broughton, the gardens were past their heyday. Choked with yellow waterlilies, the moat was only 2ft/0.6m deep and had to be dredged to a depth of 6ft/2m, before it could be stocked with rainbow trout, roach, rudd and tench. Lanning Roper advised on the replanting of the Ladies Garden in 1970. The hedges of the fleur-de-lys beds are 1ft 6in/46cm high, so this ruled out all low growing plants and 'Chanelle' and 'Pink Parfait' roses were used as the infill with *Lavandula* 'Hidcote' in the circular beds. Local rabbits became so partial to the 'Pink Parfait' roses, that they had to be replaced in 1986 with 'Gruss an Aachen'.

This view of the garden and the moat beyond, was taken through a window in the Council Chamber, where secret meetings of the Parliamentarian supporters, including Lord Saye, were believed to have taken place in the 1630s. The mixed shrub borders around the formal beds are planted with old and species roses, shrubs and perennials. A sundial once used as the centrepiece, has since been replaced by an iron basket; and the camomile surround is bordered by a Victorian coping. Broad herbaceous borders run along the west wall of the castle, and self-seeded valerian *Centranthus ruber* thrives among the remnants of a crenellated wall.

Lord and Lady Saye hope one day to restore a remarkable feature created by Lady Algernon, which she modelled on a design laid out in the gardens at New College, Oxford. On the south-west lawn a living sundial made from an upright yew gnomon, cast its shadow on roman numerals depicted with carpet bedding in a semicircular bed. Broughton's most magical asset is the moat; for the colour changes with the mood of the sky and the season. Perhaps it was the yellow flags, or fleur-de-lys, along the banks which inspired the regal shapes of both the beds in the Ladies Garden and the ceiling pattern of the Great Hall?

An Elizabethan Knot

CRANBORNE MANOR

Cranborne Manor in Dorset was originally built as a hunting lodge for John I in 1207. When it was given to Robert Cecil, the first Earl of Salisbury in 1603, the house was in ruins, but it was rebuilt with additions including mullioned windows. Shortly afterwards Cecil acquired Hatfield House, where John Tradescant the elder (c1570–1638), gardener to both James I and Cecil, designed the expansive gardens. Tradescant reputedly laid out Cranborne gardens, although there is only one record of a visit in 1610.

When the present Marquess and Marchioness of Salisbury came to live at Cranborne in 1954, they inherited a yew allée and hedges as well as an elevated mount dating back to the early seventeenth century. Lady Salisbury, a gardener since childhood, avidly read books on gardening in Elizabethan and Stuart times and decided to create a series of distinct gardens at Cranborne in the style of Tradescant's time. Before planting, the hard chalk soil had to be broken down to a depth of 3ft/1m. Manure was then spread on the surface, in a three yearly cycle; with leaf mould or compost being added annually. Lady Salisbury is a firm believer in nourishing healthy plants. Natural pyrethrum and a herbal slug killer are used in preference to chemical sprays which are generally banned from the garden. Exceptions are made for controlling weeds on the long gravel drives and for eradicating invasive bindweed from the old kitchen garden. The bindweed leaves were rubbed by hand using woollen gloves (worn over a protective rubber pair) soaked in herbicide.

The gardens at Cranborne are always a delight to visit, but spring brings a special magic of its own. Carpets of wild flowers appear in uncut grass. Tradescant's practice of mixing flowers with fruit can be seen along the spring walk through the old kitchen garden. In the herb garden, rectangular peep-holes have been cut in the surrounding yew hedges allowing glimpses of the woodland scenes beyond.

Large formal parterres have long since been grassed over, but in 1971 Lady Salisbury introduced a touch of seventeenth-century formality by designing a knot garden. Measuring 80 × 30ft/24 × 9m, it was laid out beneath the library from where the design is best appreciated. The four quarters of the rectangular garden surround a circular bed with a corkscrew-shaped box in the centre. All the beds are bordered by 6in/15cm high box edges; some have diamond or square box-edged compartments. The knot is infilled with plants of Tradescant's time, such as lady tulips *Tulipa clusiana*, old pinks and rose plantain *Plantago major* 'Rosularis'; while crown imperials *Fritillaria imperialis*, and double sweet rocket *Hesperis matronalis* give the knot a third dimension. The statue of St Rocco standing at the head of the knot, is insulated from frost by a blanket of bracken covered in hessian. The box gives form to the knot all year round, enlivened in spring and summer by scattered colour from the flowers. When the beech trees flush out a delicate green in May, they echo the colour of the knot.

Since this garden was made, Lady Salisbury has expanded her enthusiastic links with Tradescant by creating a larger knot garden at Hatfield House and by becoming President of The Tradescant Trust, based at the church of St Mary-at-Lambeth in London, where Tradescant and his son are buried.

Neatly clipped box defines the geometric pattern of the knot garden. 21 May 1986

96

A Victorian Style

LANHYDROCK

On the western slope of the upper Fowey Valley in Cornwall, lies Lanhydrock, a 150-acre park with the remnants of a 1657 sycamore avenue and a fine 1857 double beech avenue leading up to the two-storeyed gatehouse. The large informal garden on the hillside behind the church and house, contains a notable collection of magnolias and hardy hybrid rhododendrons. Five large magnolias—two *M. veitchii*, one *M. campbellii* and two *M. c. mollicomata*—all planted in 1933, are particularly striking when they flower in early spring.

In complete contrast, surrounding the house is the formal garden with many fine upright yews, which look most impressive when viewed in the early morning light against the sun streaming through thin mist. At one time, this garden was enclosed by high walls, but these were pulled down in the eighteenth century. The existing low battlemented stone walls were designed by Sir George Gilbert Scott in 1857, when the terraces were constructed facing the east and north fronts of the house. Between the north side of the house and the church, a Victorian-style parterre was laid out in 1857 and in 1935 to commemorate George V's silver jubilee. A 3ft/90cm high box hedge was added to encompass the forty-four small beds in a variety of shapes edged with dwarf box *Buxus sempervirens* 'Suffructicosa' set in a lawn.

Twice a year the bedding plants in the parterre are changed, with some variation in the colour scheme from one year to another. By August, the head gardener, Peter Borlase, has already planned his spring colour schemes. In 1987, he used *Myosotis* as the base, with red, pink or yellow tulips growing through the blue carpet; each bed having tulips of a single colour. In such a windswept site, he finds the *Myosotis* help to support the tulip stems. At the end of May, each bed is then filled with the same kind of plant of a uniform colour; although in 1987 the abnormally cold soil inhibited any growth of the seedlings until a month after planting. In 1987, *Begonia semperflorens*, *Impatiens* 'Accent' and *Ageratum* 'Blue Champion' were used for the parterre infill. (Like several blue flowers, *Ageratum* reflects infra-red wavelengths invisible to our eyes, but recorded by colour film. Hence these flowers appear magenta instead of a true blue colour.) As Lanhydrock remains open all year, immediately the first frost comes, the summer planting is removed so the spring bedding can go in.

The splendid bronze urns, originating from the Château de Bagatelle, are no longer planted since the acidic soil (pH 4.5) etched into the bronze. However, plastic inserts are now used inside bronze urns near the gatehouse, planted for several years with ivy leaved geraniums. Peter Borlase is contemplating changing to a more compact planting such as *Sempervirens* or sedums, so the shape of the urns is not obscured by overhanging stems. The rectangular box-edged beds between the house and the gatehouse are planted with roses including 'Escapade', 'Margaret Merril', 'Pink Fairy', 'Elsie Poulsen' and, best of all, 'Bright Smile' which is resistant to black spot and mildew. When Peter Borlase first came to Lanhydrock the parterre had 5ft/1.5m high 'Frensham' roses—a scale of planting which was quite unsuitable for such small beds. The pattern of the brightly coloured beds adds welcome colour to the sombre granite house but is best viewed from windows in the magnificent long gallery.

A Victorian style parterre planted with summer bedding viewed from the long gallery. 16 August 1987

View from library window of the Great Parterre at Drummond Castle.
10 August 1986

98

A Spectacular Parterre

DRUMMOND CASTLE

*L*ike many Scottish castles, Drummond stands high on a rocky outcrop. An inner courtyard leads to a walled terrace with arguably the most spectacular view of any formal garden in Britain. Below, a vast parterre spreads out in the form of an outsize St Andrew's cross with elongated diagonals, measuring 1000ft/305m long by 300ft/91m wide and covering an area of more than 6 acres. It follows the natural contours falling some 20ft/6m from west to east. This parterre is larger, and the terracing more elaborate, than those created by the second Earl of Perth in the seventeenth century. He commissioned John Mylne to design and build a sundial in 1630, as the focus to the original parterre. The obelisk-like sundial has fifty faces telling the time in most European capitals—the seventeenth-century equivalent to the 24-hour clocks of modern airports. The undulating white stripes beneath the sundial represent the waves on the Drummond coat of arms. Throughout most of the eighteenth century the family was in exile, so the garden had become a wilderness by the nineteenth century.

The precise date when the present parterre was laid out is not known, although it was almost certainly after the spectacular terracing began in 1822, probably in the 1830s, possibly by Lewis Kennedy with additions by his son, George. A painting hanging inside the Castle depicting Queen Victoria's visit to Drummond in 1842, and a photograph in Inigo Trigg's 1902 edition of *Formal Gardens in England and Scotland* taken by Charles Latham, both show the triangular beds packed with herbaceous plants. The photograph also shows the areas now covered with grass or gravel were infilled with clipped shrubs including laurels and rhododendrons.

During the Second World War, the shrubs grew unchecked and in the 1950s the parterre was restored by the Countess of Ancaster, assisted by Robert Donaldson who was head gardener from 1949–1964. Over a period of two years, rhododendrons were uprooted and the grounds ploughed and relevelled. The box edging, which was planted along many of the walkways, tends to suffer damage in severe winters. The diagonals are bordered by *Anaphalis triplinervis* which tolerates being trampled in winter, yet grows quickly in spring and contrasts well with the green turf. *Lavandula angustifolia* 'Hidcote' is used to border the three main walkways running across the width of the parterre. Statues, upright green conifers and a variety of clipped purple and golden-leaved trees provide height to the parterre, in which the restrained planting gives a more open feeling than earlier this century.

Islay Allan, who came to Drummond as head gardener in 1965, explains, 'The form of the parterre is maintained throughout the year by the box, turf and gravel. Additional colour appears when *Acer palmatum* 'Atropurpureum', A 'Osakazuki' and purple-leaved plum *Prunus cerastifera* 'pissardii' leaf out and in summer when lavender and roses—including 'Iceberg', 'Allgold' and 'Evelyn Fison', bloom. We always aimed for the colour to peak during August and September when the late Lord and Lady Ancaster were in residence.' Lord Ancaster particularly enjoyed the vista illustrated here from the elevated windows of his library, remarking, 'The nice thing about this garden is that you can see every part of it without taking a step out of doors'.

ENCLOSED GARDENS

ORIGINALLY man enclosed his land as a means of defence; indeed, East African Masai still use spiny acacia to contain their cattle and goats at night inside their *boma*. Plants, however, were not grown in enclosures until nomadic tribes stopped their peripatetic lifestyle and become more settled.

Persian gardens were initially developed within walls to provide protection from the hot arid climate; irrigation produced a microclimate in which lush growths of flowers, fruits and trees flourished in the relatively cool atmosphere. These gardens provided the inspiration for the evolution of Indian, and later on Moorish and Spanish gardens, where water was all important.

Excavations at Pompei, showed how the Romans brought their town gardens into the centre of the house where they became the focal point of family life. The central courtyard, known as the *atrium* was surrounded on all sides by colonnades—the forerunner of the cloistered courtyards in monasteries (p57) and cathedrals, obliterating the noise and bustle of the streets outside. *Trompe l'oeil* murals were painted on the walls of Pompeiian town gardens to create the illusion of a view outside; while a new window was sometimes made in a wall overlooking a neighbour's attractive garden.

Long before knots were created beneath windows of royal apartments (p12), herbers were laid out in enclosed gardens, as John Harvey relates in *Mediaeval Gardens*: 'In 1236 Henry III had a window with opening glass casements fitted in the Queen's suite [overlooking a courtyard at Windsor Castle] with covered alleyways and a herber in the centre.'

The concept of the courtyard or patio, so popular in Moorish gardens in Spain, was taken across the Atlantic to Mexico and South America by the early settlers, where it was always closely associated with the house.

Today, enclosed gardens offer not only shelter, security and privacy, but also a wide range of microclimates. The gardens of The Cloisters, New York's City Museum of Medieval Art, admirably illustrate the varied microclimates which can be created within a walled garden even in a temperate climate. Remains of ruins from European churches, castles and monasteries have been used to create the modern building in a medieval style. Espaliered fruit trees grow on warm south-facing walls; ferns and primulas thrive in shady, moist corners, while tubs of orange and fig trees stand out in the centre of the courtyard.

Additional warmth can be achieved in temperate gardens by building one wall inside another. The double walled garden at Luffness in Scotland, now unique in Britian, was erected by French prisoners of war in 1822 in the style of a French *jardin clos*. Within the diamond-shaped inner wall, the first apricots ripened in Scotland while the fig planted to commemorate the victory at Waterloo still flourishes.

The design and style are particularly important when creating a garden in a restricted space, if an air of claustrophobic clutter is to be avoided. In urban settings where a garden can be approached only via the house, many owners design it specifically to be seen from the windows. When Russell Page was commissioned to design a garden no bigger in area than the house itself, he treated the whole space as a large room with the sky as a ceiling. Green hedges or interwoven climbing plants were the walls and paving, lawn and flower beds, the carpet.

Often the layout of a small enclosed garden can be appreciated only from a high viewpoint, such as a window in an upper floor; five of the six gardens featured in this chapter have been photographed from an elevated window.

A Thameside View

29 DEODAR ROAD, LONDON

After the severe and prolonged 1985–6 winter, spring came late to Britain so that, even in the south, by mid-April little was in bloom in gardens apart from some *Narcissus*, species tulips and a few magnolias. It was therefore a particularly welcome sight to walk from the front, through a narrow side passage, to the rear of a Thameside town garden in Putney on a sunny morning to be greeted by the striking pink flowers of *Magnolia campbelli mollicomata*. Planted in 1957 as a seedling from Caerhays garden in Cornwall—famed for its *Magnolia* and *Camellia* collections—it was twenty years before it flowered, but has done so annually ever since. A spray of flowers from this tree won first prize for large-flowered magnolias at the Royal Horticultural Society's 1987 spring show.

Invariably, spectacular magnolias towering 20ft/6m or more, have to be viewed from ground level against the sky. Although a blue backcloth complements white and pink flowers well, the full beauty of individual flowers and, especially the heart of the flower, cannot be fully appreciated unless seen from an adjacent elevated view-point or viewed through binoculars. This magnolia was planted quite close to the house, so that the view from the 15ft/4.5m first floor would be on a level with the flowers for many years. Visible from neighbouring gardens to left and right, as well as from the river, it enlivens the Thameside vista at a time of year when relatively little colour is apparent in the gardens. Directly behind the magnolia is a *Robinia pseudoacacia* festooned with a *Vitis pulchra* which provides a colourful elevated screen in the autumn. As the magnolia blooms begin to fade, the first of more than seventy camellias come into flower; notably the dark red *Camellia japonica* 'Konron Koku'. All these, as well as many other shrubs, roses and herbaceous plants, have been planted by the present owners in their north-facing garden overshadowed by the house. During almost three decades they have found by trial and error which plants flourish. Alpines and azaleas do not, whereas camellias are clearly very much at home. Hardy crane's-bills *Geranium* spp. are underplanted beneath *rugosa* roses while many wild flowers are encouraged to spread as ground cover beneath the shrubs.

Beyond, there is a fascinating kaleidoscope of river traffic accompanying the rise and fall of the tides. Passing oarsmen, pleasure steamers and power boats, move up and down the river while fishermen and beachcombers, who operate from the banks, provide an ever-changing view of the river from this unusual town garden. It is surprising anyone ever manages to tear themselves away to make the descent down a spiral staircase to work in the garden.

Although the garden is noted for its camellias, there are other flowering shrubs of interest such as *Viburnum carlesii* and *Osmanthus decorus* early in the year; while in late summer *Buddleia* × *weyeriana* flowers attract butterflies and dreary winter days are enlivened by pendulous racemes of fragrant yellow *Mahonia japonica* flowers.

Owners of estates with trees bearing large showy flowers on high branches might well be inspired to build an adjacent elevated viewing mount to allow a greater appreciation of the form and colour of flowers close-up; as has been achieved so successfully in this modest-sized garden, packed with interesting plant associations.

Magnolia campbellii mollicomata *flowering in a Thameside garden.* 13 April 1986

A Living Jigsaw

THE CROSSING HOUSE

Passengers travelling on the King's Cross to Cambridge line who happen to look out of the window near Shepreth station are in for a treat, for the railside is alive with colourful plants. Each year, the colour extends further up the line towards the station as Margaret and Douglas Fuller expand their quarter-acre garden on both sides of the railway.

Shortly after they moved to the Crossing House in 1959, their triangular garden, bordered by a road on one side and a railway line on the other, was typical of any small suburban garden backing on to a railway. 'Cheap and cheerful' plants such as *Forsythia*, hybrid tea roses and delphiniums provided instant colour amongst the children's sand pit. Ten years later, as Margaret Fuller's knowledge of plants increased, most of the originals were uprooted. Now, well into their third decade as practicing gardeners, the Fullers have amassed over five thousand choice plants in their small garden. Margaret Fuller favours plants which also embellish the garden before or after they flower, and she grows parsley specifically for its textured leaves. Plants which tolerate cutting after flowering are a bonus, since they provide space for others to come into their prime, ensuring the living jigsaw puzzle constantly changes. Any plant which outgrows its allotted space is removed. Special favourites are winter-flowering plants, among them eighteen different *Hamamelis*. In spring, the garden is a sea of bulbs, followed by a succession of alpines and flowering dwarf shrubs. Late colour comes from autumn crocuses, annuals sown in July and late-flowering *Lilium speciosum*. The alkaline soil does not deter the Fullers from growing calcifuge plants—three hundred of them have been planted in pots, and their coloured rims are camouflaged with pieces of Westmorland stone. Douglas Fuller looks after two heated greenhouses full of non-hardy plants and a cool house packed with alpines and some four hundred auriculas.

Statues and water features are strategically placed throughout the garden. A discarded copper from the house became the liner for the first pool; while a low box hedge encircles an expanse of stones and fossils on to which a fountain bubbles, accentuating the colours of the stones.

In January and February, Margaret Fuller weeds beside the railway line, for, 'In spring and summer when I work constantly in the garden, the railside verges must look after themselves.' A recent trackside feature is a delightful knot garden inspired by the one at Cranborne Manor (p95). In July 1987, huge drifts of double opium and double Shirley poppies and self-seeded rosebay willow herb *Epilobium angustifolium*, camouflage a pile of bindweed roots, telegraph poles and wires.

For safety reasons, railway tracks must be kept weed free, but spray from the weed killer train has not only destroyed the cultivated railside margins, but, on occasions, strayed into the Fullers' garden. However, after the Crossing House garden was featured on television in 1984, hand-held sprays are now used.

The Fullers' garden exemplifies how, with careful selection of the plants and skilful planting, a small garden in the most unpromising of sites can become a masterpiece. Nothing is left to chance. Photographs are taken at monthly intervals of each bed so that improvements can be made to the design and plant associations.

The railside garden at Shepreth extends along the line. 8 July 1987

A Leafy Patchwork

BROOK COTTAGE

Rough pasture covering a steeply sloping hillside and falling towards a valley that funnels the south-west wind, is not the most promising of sites on which to develop a garden. In the Oxfordshire village of Alkerton this has been achieved in little more than two decades by the combined talents of an architect and a plantswoman. David and Kathleen Hodges' constant devotion to detail whilst keeping the overall design in mind, clearly shows throughout their four-acre garden.

The 30ft/9m × 36ft/10.8m courtyard enclosed on three sides by the L-shaped house and a converted barn, is particularly attractive in early summer when clumps of hostas and *Alchemilla mollis* have grown up to form spreading crowns, just before *Campanula portenschlagiana*, mimulus and astilbes begin to flower. Seen from the top of steps which lead down to the courtyard, this patchwork of varied green hues created by the leaves of hostas, *Astrantia major* 'Variegata' and *Filipendula ulmaria* 'Aurea', is attractively offset against the sombre flagstones. The absence of any slug damage to the hosta leaves is achieved by spraying with a liquid slug killer once the first shoots begin to break the ground.

A flagged courtyard would appear to be an unpromising site for growing shade and moisture-loving hostas, but this apparently arid situation is deceptive. The Hodges' initially attempted to grow typical sun-loving rock plants such as aubretias, but met with failure. It was only when a marsh marigold *Caltha palustris* appeared, they realized that the subsoil was kept wet by underground watercourses and by rain water running down the steep grassy slope straight on to the courtyard. A Regency marble pot planted with half-hardy plants including *Cosmos atrosanguineus*, *Felicia* 'Santa Anika', *Helichrysum petiolatum* 'Variegatum' and *Lotus bertholetii* add both height and contrast to the leafy clumps.

The courtyard is one small feature of a garden with many distinct parts, all planted with a plethora of unusual plants. From a formal central terrace, extends a series of interconnecting gardens bounded by hedges. Leading from these are more informal and open areas which extend the garden towards the adjacent natural landscape. Water features include an ornamental pond and bog garden fed by natural springs in a depression where cattle once came to drink. When the garden was levelled for a lawn, an old stone culvert was discovered carrying spring water to the brook which flows along the western boundary. This water supply was tapped to feed stone rills made around three sides of the lawn. A serpentine lake provides an expanse of calm water which effectively mirrors the surrounding hills and sky, broken only by an island deliberately sparsely planted.

Sadly, an infestation of honey fungus has extended its underground rhizomorphs, resembling black bootlaces, to several choice trees and shrubs. This no doubt originated in the hedges dividing the old fields. Removal of infected roots and sterilization of the soil with formaldehyde will never completely eradicate this fungus.

A judicious selection of plants is included in separate white, yellow and pink–blue borders. A striking feature of the garden is the informal planting of over a hundred shrub roses on a hillside where space allows even the largest species to develop their full potential. An alpine scree bed, completed in 1985, is the latest feature to be added to a garden of great interest throughout the year.

Lush clumps of hostas and Alchemilla mollis *enliven an Oxfordshire courtyard. 3 June 1987*

A Sunken Garden

CHENIES MANOR

The Manor House in the Buckinghamshire village of Chenies is steeped in history. Parts of the house date back to the thirteenth century when it was owned by the Cheyne family and used by Edward I. In the 1520s the estate passed to the Russells (earls and dukes of Bedford) who owned it for four centuries. The first Earl of Bedford hosted Henry VIII, Anne Boleyn and Kathryn Howard at Chenies in 1534, and the second Earl entertained Elizabeth I. After the Civil War, the Bedfords moved to Woburn Abbey in Bedfordshire and Chenies was let to tenant farmers. By the time Colonel and Mrs Macleod Matthews bought the Manor in 1955, all trace of the 4-acre Tudor Great Garden had long since gone; the front courtyard was partly relegated to chickens, while laurel hedges dominated the Little Gardens to the rear of the house.

After removing the laurels, the Macleod Matthews found a depression corresponding with a small garden marked on an early plan, so in 1956 they decided to lay out a sunken garden modelled on the Tudor Pond Garden at Hampton Court. A low brick wall (now camouflaged with ivy and topped with a trellis) was built as a boundary to the lawn and the sunken garden. Later on, an evergreen cypress avenue with taller columns of dark yew, was planted both as a shelter belt to the south winds and a living wall to the enclosed gardens.

The narrow grass terraces, York stone paths, central oval pool and box topiary provide a solid framework to the sunken garden throughout the year. Perennials with distinct foliage such as irises, hostas, Solomon's seal and bergenias give living form to the succession of flowers from spring through to late summer. After the spring bulbs have faded, a mauve and white phase develops in midsummer followed by warm golds, oranges and reds. Hostas, *Nepeta* and *Campanula glomerata* provide mauves, brightened by lime yellow *Alchemilla mollis* and white *Campanula latiloba*.

Elizabeth Macleod Matthews, the inspiration behind the new plantings, comments after repeated defoliation of Solomon's seal by sawfly larvae, 'the only cure is to spray the underside of the leaves with a systemic fluid a week after flowering'. She loves the frothy *Alchemilla* flowers, but once they flop on the lawns, they are cut and dried, in a specially designed loft, for the shop.

From early childhood, Elizabeth has loved plants and gardening. After laboriously digging deep trenches for her sweet peas, she produced prize-winning blooms and has grown them ever since. The white garden, originally a topiary garden with herbs, still contains large yew birds on box plinths. Two of the yews planted in shallow soil above 'secret' passages need additional water in dry weather. Beyond the formal garden, a physic garden contains herbs, and a range of perfumed, dyestuff and medicinal plants.

Elizabeth also has a keen interest in garden history. Using the layout of a 'labyrinth' depicted in a 1580 painting at Woburn Abbey, she has had an exact replica recreated as a turf maze at Chenies. As well as initiating a permanent exhibition illustrating the evolution of gardening in England since Roman times, she runs day courses on flower arranging at Chenies and hosts a school of garden design. Her Little Garden is in keeping with the late medieval and Tudor home, although the plants used are not limited to this period.

The sunken garden on a midsummer's evening. 28 June 1987

An Oasis in a Desert

*H*idden behind a high brick frontage, in a Philadelphia side street, lies a gem of a city garden. Originally used as parking lots, this L-shaped garden extends back 110ft/33m and the 32ft/10m width broadens out behind the house. The inspiration behind this oasis in a desert is Ann McPhail, a lecturer in oriental art and a garden designer. After plans were drawn up in 1971, the construction and planting of the connecting gardens took five years to complete. An intriguing aspect of the design is the changes in elevation that have been achieved in such a small space.

The whole garden is held together by curving brick paths painstakingly laid by Ann McPhail's husband, while she checked, and modified where necessary, the flowing lines from an upper window. The brick walkways tie the whole garden together and subtle changes in their levels are not merely aesthetic, they also help to solve drainage problems in an enclosed garden. This picture, taken from the third floor, shows how the paths lead the eye from one part of the garden to another. Many of the plants—hostas, hollies and junipers—have been chosen for their varied texture. Additional colour is provided in spring by bulbs, dicentras, ajuga, azaleas and a flowering crab apple. A succession of perennials bloom in early summer with wax begonias and impatiens; chrysanthemums provide colour until mid-fall.

The herb garden in front of the pavilion has a distinct Japanese influence. Large grey stones, inset in a pebble mixture, function as stepping stones, while the rounded water-worn stones collected from rivers in Maine are purely ornamental. Spreading over the gravel and stones are mat-forming thymes, used as a substitute for mosses unable to survive temperatures up to 37 °C.

Air pollution and dehydration of the soil are two problems encountered by a city gardener in Philadelphia. For nine months of the year—from March–November—Ann McPhail waters her garden. All plants are fertilized in the spring, some again in the fall and shrubs are pruned four times in the summer.

Although the garden walls and nearby commercial buildings cast shadows across the garden early and late in the day, a surprisingly wide selection of plants thrive on the walls. Vines are an obvious choice, but ivies, cotoneasters, euonymus and the hardy orange, *Poncirus trifoliata*, are all trained as espaliers. An open grown specimen of the Atlas cedar, *Cedrus atlantica glauca* is capable of reaching 120 ft/36m tall—quite impractical for an enclosed garden. Here, the growth form has been transformed by planting the conifer beside a wall, and the leader tied horizontally so the side branches cascade down like an evergreen waterfall. The wall-coverers, trees and shrubs help to muffle persistent city sounds.

A mixture of hardy and tropical plants are grown in the small pond. Emergent pickerel weed, *Pontederia cordata* survives the winter, but the floating water hyacinth, *Eichhornia crassipes* is renewed each spring. Fan-tail goldfish provide mobile colour in the pool all year round. The problem of trespassing cats intent on poaching has been solved by edging the pool with ivy; the springiness of the ivy stems tends to unsettle any cat that stalks towards her pool.

Ann McPhail's philosophy that 'all gardens should be created for year-round interest, especially a city garden constantly on view', is borne out by her own garden.

Brick walkways connect varied features in a Philadelphia garden. 13 October 1986

Evening light reveals the
secrets of a suburban
Leeds garden.
26 July 1986

A Secret Garden

LEEDS SUBURBAN GARDEN

The front garden of Joe and Frieda Brown's suburban Leeds house is colourful and typical of anyone who loves flowers; but nowhere, as you approach the front, is there any hint of the secret garden beyond the back door. Here, over a period of two decades, they have transformed a 78ft/24m long narrow plot into a garden renowned in the north of England and, after being featured on television, visited widely.

The Browns insist their creation is a joint achievement: Joe drew on his civil engineering experience when constructing the framework, the small pool near the house, the patio area, the alpine garden, the archway and the raised pond; while Frieda's art college training and eye for colour combinations ensure that judicious planting provides colour from early spring to late autumn.

The time, energy, love and devotion that they put into transforming a flat barren strip bisected by a cinder track is all the more remarkable when Frieda admits the sum total of their combined gardening knowledge at the outset 'would have covered a pin head'. Being both resourceful, and opportunistic, they were not slow to take advantage of a disused quarry nearby. Painstakingly, they collected rocks for the alpine garden by pushing wheelbarrow loads up the hill.

Straight lines of alternating colour are abhorred by the Browns, instead they use flowing lines of grass, stone and water throughout the garden to lead you on from one unexpected delight to another. In this plantsman's garden, a happy mixture of shrubs, perennials and annuals thrive harmoniously together. Frieda likes using annuals because 'they add vivacity and fill the gaps between the perennials'. She raises both annuals and perennials from seed; although she admits as she grows older, she becomes impatient when waiting for the perennials to flower.

Frieda explains their creation: 'We have never drawn up plans. I go out, sit and ruminate and, suddenly see what I have to do. My main method is to work by instinct. The limited space meant we had to consider every square inch. If a plant does not come up to expectations, we dig it up and give it away. After much trial and error the garden emerged as a series of small rooms at a time when we had not even heard of, let alone seen, Hidcote. The main problem was hiding the surrounding bricks and concrete—what better way than by creating living curtains of climbing plants?'

Frieda likes 'ornaments to be part of the garden without distracting from the planting'. A white plastic bird bath was transformed by coating it with a mix of white and black paint so as to resemble grey stone. A cast iron urn spied in an antique shop caked in white lime wash was renovated by gradually chipping away to reveal the details, and then painted a Regency green to blend in with the garden. The urn is planted with South African and West Australian annuals, with *Abutilon* as a centrepiece.

The Browns are justly proud of their small garden which they have completely transformed by planting some thousand different species of plants. However, even Frieda was quite overcome on a summer's day in 1981 when some four hundred visitors turned up after an article appeared in a national newspaper. She suspects it may have been the reference to their camomile lawn being a feature they shared in common with The Queen!

THE ORIENTAL INFLUENCE

ANCIENT Chinese gardens include the vast imperial parks such as the Summer Palace near Beijing and Bi shu shan zhuang at Chengde, as well as the private gardens built by landowners, aristocrats and rich merchants. The restored classical gardens in Suzhou represent the style of private gardens in south China. Here the concentration of rich, well educated men, the subtropical climate and the abundance of water and rocks favoured the creation of a plethora of small gardens between 1522–1796.

Both Taoist worship of nature and Buddhist philosophy influenced the development of naturalistic gardens. Painters and poets tended to lay out gardens designed to replicate natural landscapes of mountains, hills and pools in miniature. A typical 1–2 mu garden (a mu equals 0.677 hectare), was divided into a series of courtyards, linked with winding paths and corridors to create a variety of scenes. Open doorways (circular moon gates, hexagonal or vase-shaped openings) or open windows with or without latticework (p124), break up the monotonous expanse of walls and provide glimpses of what lies beyond.

Illusions, created by means of differential scale and juxtaposition of light and shadow, recur throughout the gardens. For example, at the Blue Waves Pavilion (Cang Lang Ting) an impression of increased size is achieved by borrowing the scenery beyond the garden walls where a long corridor winding beside a stream outside, links the 'water' outside with the 'mountains' inside the garden.

Pavilions were specifically built for contemplating views of the garden. The significance of windows in houses and pavilions is summed up in the Chinese proverb as being '. . . the eyes of a house or a pavilion. Without them the place is blind, even dead; with them it comes to life.'

In overcrowded modern Japanese cities, few can afford the luxury of enough space for a private garden, although in small courtyards or *tsuboniwa*, a few plants and ornaments can be used most effectively. On the smallest of balconies room is made for miniature tray-gardens (*bon-kai*) and dwarf trees or *bonsai*. Traditional landscaping skills are seen in temple and palace gardens in Kyoto. These are full of symbolic features and lack any suggestion of symmetry and formality. Pine trees are trained into precise shapes by pruning and manipulation with wire. Areas of grass, moss or sand may be punctuated with precisely positioned rocks.

During the fifteenth century, after tea was introduced to Zen monasteries, tea-houses were built in gardens for the ritual tea ceremony or *cha-no-yu*. The stone lantern, stepping stones and the stone water basin were three features introduced to the tea garden or *cha-niwa* by the tea-masters early in the sixteenth century. Unlike the pavilions built with windows framing garden scenes outside, tea-houses had their windows covered with rice paper so there would be no distractions from the outside view.

In the mid-eighteenth century, a fashion for chinoiserie buildings—houses, pagodas and bridges—appeared in British gardens, but it was not until early this century that Japanese gardens were created in Britain and Ireland. The moon gate continues to appear in a few western gardens. One was used at West Green House in Hampshire to frame the view from the *jardin potager* up some steps to a nymphaeum, but by 1987 overgrown shrub roses blocked the vista. Beatrix Farrand incorporated a moon gate into her 1920s design for the Rockefeller Garden in Maine. She also designed the garden at Dumbarton Oaks in Washington DC, where a quatrefoil peach blossom aperture frames a view from the Fountain Terrace.

Shades of Autumn

THE JAPANESE GARDEN AT COTTERED

Early this century, at much the same time as the Japanese garden was laid out at Tully, in Ireland (p122), Herbert Goode, a wealthy glass and china merchant, was planning a series of dells and shady walks in his Hertfordshire garden. However, after visiting Japan in 1905, he was so captivated with the gardens there, that he bought back several stone lanterns and ornaments in the ships he used for exporting his china. After a second Japanese visit a few years later, he directed the laying out of a three-quarter-acre Japanese garden at Cottered. A landscape in miniature, with mountains, lakes and waterfalls, was created from three flat fields bordered by hedges without any natural water.

From 1923–6 Seyemon Kusumoto advised on the finishing touches, notably the positioning of bridges and other buildings. At this time, it was regarded as one of the most authentic Japanese gardens in Britain. Twenty-one gardeners maintained it, together with the rest of the $4\frac{1}{2}$-acre garden. Herbert Goode had no children, so after he and his wife died, the estate was split up and sold. Successive owners have moved ornaments elsewhere, so the Japanese garden is now somewhat depleted. Since the present owners Susan and Graeme Woodhatch came in 1985, bridges and buildings have been extensively restored and missing ornaments retrieved.

The present head gardener, Mr William Wilds, has worked at Cottered since 1969, looking after the remaining $3\frac{1}{2}$ acres with only one assistant, Mark Skipp. Six copies of the Cottered garden book were produced in 1933 describing and illustrating all the main features. The Tea House (restored in 1986), together with the Sacred Bridge which crosses a narrow part of Fox Lake (Kitsune-ike), were built in Japan. The bridge is modelled on the famous sacred bridge (Shin-kyo) at Nikko where the exteriors of all the wooden structures are protected from the continual rains and mist by brightly coloured lacquers. All the bridges at Cottered have recently been restored and finished in vermilion, and from almost any viewpoint in the garden at least one bridge can be seen in complete contrast to the evergreen foliage. When the maples turn in autumn, they echo the colour of the bridges and an additional autumn shade comes from the bright yellow leaves of *Ginkgo biloba*—a sacred tree in Japan.

Flowers also contribute isolated patches of contrasting colour to the garden. In spring, after the Japanese cherries have faded, long purple wisteria racemes fall from a canopy covering a stepping stone path; later on, a clump of white *Anemone japonica* contrasts well against a red bridge. In midsummer, *Iris kaempferi* brings colour to waterside margins, while pink and white water lily flowers open out above the still water. Koi carp provide mobile colour as they swim lazily in the larger pond.

Scattered throughout the garden are huge stones, some weighing over a ton, brought back from Japan by Mr Goode. A roofed entrance gate, *torii*, stone and bronze lanterns and sculpted herons can still be seen at Cottered. The perimeter fence to the Japanese garden has several apertures sparsely decorated with bamboo, through which the garden can be glimpsed. Although many of the original plants, including eight kinds of bamboo, have died or been dug up, the garden still retains some of the basic elements of a Japanese design which has developed albeit in an English climate.

View from upper storey of Japanese guest house. 2 October 1986

116

FAN-SHAPED WINDOWS

ABOVE: *Palm framed by fan window, Yuantong Temple, Kunming. 22 April 1985*

RIGHT: *A fan window in ice garden, Harbin. 7 February 1987*

Fan-shaped Windows

TWO CHINESE GARDENS

*A*pertures in the walls of classical Chinese gardens function as peep-holes providing tantalizing glimpses of the garden beyond. The fan is a simple, but effective shape often used as an aperture in Chinese gardens. The upper and lower curves repeat the undulating top of a cloud wall.

Many of China's temple gardens also feature windows, often within corridor walls, invariably tucked away from the main tourist thoroughfare. Bordering Burma, Laos and Vietnam is China's most south-westerly province, Yunnan. Early in March, temple gardens in the provincial capital, Kunming, are enlivened with magnolias and camellias. At other times of year, potted plants are brought in, notably chrysanthemums in autumn. Evergreens and trees planted in beds may be offset by a red wall or framed by a window.

The main attractions of the Buddhist Yuantong Temple, built in the middle of the Tang Dynasty, are an octagonal pavilion in the centre of a lake and a temple with a pair of multi-coloured dragons. Possibly overlooked by many tourists, are the windows which pierce a gallery, flanking a courtyard. In 1985, a fan window here effectively framed a palm growing in a small bed beyond the wall. The unlit wall appears grey in contrast to the sunlit palm and the wall beyond. Plants growing up from ground level will not always be perfectly positioned in the picture; whereas potted plants can be raised or lowered on a support so that they remain perfectly framed.

Two thousand miles away from Kunming and north of Beijing, the capital of China, lies the ice city of Harbin. There, winter lasts from October to the end of April, with temperatures remàining well below freezing from November to March, and in January they can plunge as low as −38°C. After being disbanded during the Cultural Revolution, the traditional Ice Lantern Festival was revived in 1982. Huge blocks of ice, cut from the frozen Songhua River, are used to make the ice sculptures; the designs being drawn to scale on paper and created using shaped blocks frozen together by injecting water between them. Planes, chisels, knives and grinding wheels are used to sculpt the ice into a variety of designs, which change each year but tend to be traditional Chinese symbolic shapes. In 1987, the sculptures in Zhaoling Park included a pagoda, bridges, a garden, a boat, a dragon, a goldfish and, since it was the year of the rabbit, numerous ice rabbits.

During the day, the sculptures look most effective when rim lit by the early or late sun. By night, they are completely transformed by coloured electric lights glowing from within. Traditional Chinese garden art was the inspiration behind the ice garden, with ice walls perforated by circular and fan-shaped windows looking on to an ice lantern in the inner courtyard. Maybe the Chinese see the ghostly silhouettes of people inside the ice-walled garden, as symbolizing the much prized water-worn rocks so precisely placed in their traditional gardens. In the past, pathways to houses used to be lined with smaller ice decorations made by pouring water over real flowers, fish or crabs in moulds so they became frozen inside the ice. Living blossom will not withstand exposure to freezing air temperatures, so sprays of artificial blossom decorate the favourite ice sculptures used as backdrops for photographing family or friends.

A Glazed Scene

THE SUMMER PALACE

*E*xamples of ornamental unglazed windows with decorative internal latticework are illustrated elsewhere in this book (p124 and p126). A variation on the Chinese window theme can be seen at the Summer Palace north-west of Beijing, where the Imperial households used to reside during the summer months. The basic plan of the Summer Palace dates back some eight centuries. The main features in the 692-acre park are Longevity Hill to the north, which looks down onto Kunming Lake to the south. In summer, the lake is used for boating; in winter when it freezes over, people can skate and take short cuts across it.

In 1860 the Palace was looted and burnt to the ground by British and French troops, only to be reconstructed and enlarged by the Empress Dowager Cixi, utilizing funds designated for the navy. Renamed *Yi he yuan* (the Garden of Good Health and Harmony), the Summer Palace was destroyed in 1900 by Allied Forces, but restored three years later. Once again the Empress spared nothing to rebuild the Palace. After it became a public park in 1924 there followed a gradual period of destruction and decay. This time, it took more than thirty years to restore the Palace which now attracts millions of visitors each year.

Pavilions, pagodas, temples, covered walkways and bridges are among the traditional architectural features to be seen at the Summer Palace. Two long, and several side, corridors adjacent to Kunming Lake are perforated by a series of double-glazed windows. Each long corridor has sixteen distinctly shaped windows, including a circle, a fan (p118), a pentagon, a hexagon, an octagon and a stylized leaf. Viewed from the lakeside, each window has an outer surround painted black. On one window this black surround is shaped as a teapot, complete with a handle and spout.

On the outside of each pane facing on to the covered walkway, is a flower painting. Unfortunately, several of the windows are now cracked and the details of many paintings have worn off the glass, so only a few are worth photographing. This double diamond window has a painting of a potted conifer, illustrating *penjing*—the Chinese art of creating miniature trees and gardens. Penjing was practised in China many centuries before the Japanese coined the universally accepted word, *bonsai* for their miniature trees. In 1972, Chinese archaeologists discovered the tomb of Prince Zhang Huai, built in AD 706 in Shaanxi Province. Two of the murals in the tomb depict ladies-in-waiting carrying miniature potted landscapes. The earliest known illustrations of Japanese bonsai appear on a scroll dating back only some eight hundred years. Originally, miniature trees or shrubs were sought in the wild; nowadays they are nurtured from seedlings grown in shallow pots. Growth is checked by pruning both roots and shoots.

In February, the view through the double glazed window on to the frozen lake shows people walking and skating on the ice. During the summer, these windows overlook a bed of lush green lotus leaves with their elegant single pink flowers. As well as being decorative, the windows also had a useful function. The wooden frame of each inner pane was hinged, so that it could be opened and a candle placed inside the window; these glowing apertures were used to help illuminate the lake for boating parties at night.

Double glazed window with penjing *painting, overlooks Kunming Lake, The Summer Palace. 9 February 1987*

A Japanese Story

THE JAPANESE GARDENS, TULLY

The Japanese Gardens near Kildare, were devised by Colonel William Hall-Walker (later Lord Wavertree) at Tully Stud Farm where he bred racehorses and had a large alpine nursery. He brought Tassa Eida and his son Minoru over from Japan to lay out the one and a half-acre gardens from 1906–10. In common with other Japanese gardens created in Britain at the turn of the century, they did not attempt to replicate gardens in Japan; rather to represent a merging of Eastern and Western cultures. All the ornamentations associated with Japanese gardens, have been incorporated into a landscape designed to portray man's passage of life from the womb to the tomb, by means of oriental symbolism. In Japan, it is the apparently simplistic dry landscape gardens which are known for their symbolic qualities; but Colonel Hall-Walker introduced his symbolic story into a tea garden.

Before the hills, caverns, pools and waterfalls could be built, Irish labourers, under Eida's direction, collected local limestone rocks and drained a bog on a flat site. Trees, shrubs, exquisite bonsai, stone lanterns, a prefabricated tea-house and a unique model village carved out of Mount Fujiyama lava were all shipped over from Japan to embellish the landscape in miniature.

The entrance through the Gateway of Oblivion leads to a small cavern, the Cave of Birth. From here, the first steps of life lead into the dark Tunnel of Ignorance; inside, the light of Knowledge leads up the Hill of Learning. The story continues via the Engagement and Marriage Bridges, along the Honeymoon Path up to the Hill of Ambition ultimately to the Chair of Old Age to the Hill of Mourning.

Colonel Hall-Walker's stud farm became the Irish National Stud in 1945. After several decades of neglect, following Colonel Hall-Walker's departure for England in 1915, Patrick Doyle came to Tully as the horticultural adviser in 1946 and began essential restoration. The original tea-house roof made from reeds was destroyed some thirty years ago by someone burning out a wasp's nest. By the time John Colleran succeeded Patrick Doyle in 1973, the narrow paths were completely enclosed by overhanging branches, so extensive tree surgery was required to clear the paths. Colleran created a *kare san sui* (dry landscape) garden and a Zen meditation garden in the style of Ryoan-ji in Kyoto. He also increased the range of Japanese plants, which would have gained the approval of Tassa Eida, who would, no doubt have turned in his grave if he had known of the time when a traditional local gardener established hybrid tea roses and bedding plants in his garden!

Pines are an important feature in Japanese gardens, for they are a symbol of long life and happiness, but many of the Scots pines which were semi-mature when they were planted at Tully in 1910, have now grown out of all proportion to the scale of the ornaments. Early in the year, mahonias and *Camellia japonica* flower, followed by Japanese azaleas, cherries, wisteria and kerrias. Most trees are pruned each winter, notably the cherries, maples and pines.

This garden obviously gives a great deal of pleasure to the sixty thousand people who visit it each year from April to September, but such numbers can deny the solitude required for meditating the symbolic qualities of this unique and well maintained garden.

Small craggy window in cavern frames Well of Wisdom. 19 August 1987

Ornamental Lattice Windows

CHINESE GARDENS

*W*ithin a handful of restored classical gardens in Suzhou, an infinite variety of ornamental unglazed windows with decorative internal latticework can be seen. However, ornamental windows are by no means confined to these gardens and delightful variations can be seen all over China in houses, temples, parks, garden buildings and galleries.

Before glass was known in China, rice paper was used as a substitute to fill windows in houses. The paper was reinforced by patterned frames, which also served a decorative function. When lit from within, the pattern appeared as a silhouette on the paper. These frameworks were the forerunners of the open lattice windows used to pierce galleries and walls so that portions of the garden beyond the wall could be glimpsed. The amount seen depends on the intricacy of the lattice; a dense pattern with small spaces merely shows small portions of colour, typically green, rather than any discernible shapes. Like so many features of Chinese gardens, the design of the window grille may have a symbolic meaning based on one of the five blessings—longevity, riches, good health, peace of mind and love of virtue.

Among the most widespread designs used in the geometrical lattice windows of walkways, galleries and buildings in Chinese classical gardens are those based on rectilinear shapes. Small parallelograms or squares are often repeated within a large outer rectangle or square. Designs based on linked swastikas have been used in western China for two to three centuries, symbolizing the traces of Buddha's footsteps in Buddhistic art. Patterns which appear in cracked ice or waves are also stylized as window designs. The latticework may not always fill the entire aperture, especially in large rectangular picture windows which tend to have an ornate border only around the edges. When viewing such windows from inside an unlit corridor looking out into a bright sunlit garden, the lattice will appear in silhouette.

Various materials are used to make the lattice. Geometric patterns involving curving lines can be made from roof tiles, while cast bricks were used for bold simplistic designs. Mahogany was used to create the striking effect based on the interlocking design of a fishing net meshwork in the Fisherman's Garden (Wang Shi Yuan) in Suzhou. Elaborate pictorial scenes of plants and birds are created by modelling clay on a wire framework, which is then baked and painted. As in paintings, cranes—long-lived birds which symbolize longevity—are often depicted with pine trees in ornate windows as well as in courtyard mosaics. The deer is another animal used as a symbol of longevity.

The apertures themselves are also highly variable, based on both geometrical and naturalistic shapes. Quatrefoil and cinquefoil designs based on the stylized outline of petals of a peach or plum flower are widespread, used both as open apertures and outlines for decorative infills. As well as flowers, the ornamental flora of window shapes include fungi, fruits and leaves.

Modern buildings in parks continue to use traditional shapes to frame outside views. The architect I M Pei sought inspiration from traditional garden architecture for the Fragrant Hill Hotel, recently built on the outskirts of Beijing, where he used several quatrefoil windows to frame views from the main reception area to the garden (p15).

OPPOSITE: *Lingering Garden, Suzhou. 2 May 1985* OVERLEAF: *Birds and blossom, Golden Temple, Kunming. 4 March 1986*

ROCK & WATER SPECTACLES

WATER can bring magical qualities to a garden of any size. Reflections in calm water repeat the shapes of waterside plants, ornaments or buildings, while moving water introduces sound. Moats and mill-races are examples of water features which were originally functional, but are now used ornamentally. Being in such close proximity to the house, they are inevitably overlooked by windows (p29). The elevated windows of the tall pavilion, in the recently restored seventeenth-century Dutch-style water garden at Westbury Court in Gloucestershire, provide splendid views of the long canal, the rest of the garden and the river Severn beyond. In the flat Dutch landscape, painters frequently climbed high buildings to gain overviews of the countryside. At Blenheim Palace in Oxfordshire, the full design by Achille Duchêne, of the water parterre, with its single jets, cannot be appreciated from ground level, but from high up in the palace, not only can the complete design be seen, but the eye is led across the parterre and the lower water terrace to 'Capability' Brown's lake beyond. Expansive water features with copious fountains tend to be located away from the house, possibly because they are so noisy. But the lavish white plumes in the majestic water garden at the Villa d'Este at Tivoli in Italy are a key element in the grand design seen from the house standing on top of series of terraces.

One of the earliest gardens to be illustrated, appears on an Egyptian fresco c1400 BC, on the tomb of Nebamun in Thebes. It shows water lilies and waterfowl in four rectangular pools edged with papyrus. Trees, as well as date and doum palms around the pools, must have provided welcome shade in the hot climate. Although the Chinese grew water lilies in containers from AD 10, the cultivation of aquatic plants purely for aesthetic reasons is a comparatively recent trend in the West. In the enclosed Persian paradise gardens, water was used for irrigation, display, reducing high temperatures and for creating sound. Designs woven into old Persian carpets show water channels dividing the garden into quadrants. Water also played a functional role in Indian, Moorish and Spanish gardens, where fountain sprays trapped dust and cooled the air. Raised pools are a feature of Spanish gardens, where they can be framed by arches around a court. In China, the moon gate is a symbol of perfection and circular images are created by the reflection of semicircular arches supporting a bridge in clear water.

Water is also an important element in Japanese gardens; although absent from the Zen dry landscapes, the raked sand and arrangement of pebbles is designed to simulate a dry stream bed. Individual rocks are so much revered in the orient that great thought is given to their positioning. In China, the bizarre-shaped limestone rocks scoured by water erosion in Lake Tai are especially prized and pavilions were built for viewing and contemplating them.

Amongst the most novel views of water seen through windows must surely have been from inside the 80ft/24m high conservatory Whitaker Wright had built beneath the lake in Lea (now Witley) Park in Surrey at the end of the last century. From here, fish could be seen swimming past by day, while the stars and moon shone eerily through the water at night.

The most perfect integration of house, rock and water was achieved by the American architect Frank Lloyd Wright when he designed in 1937 the house known as Falling Water at Bear Run in Pennsylvania for Edgar J Kaufmann. On a riverside rock in the forest, a cantilevered house with glass walls was built out over the cascading water.

Edwardian Elegance

DYFFRYN GARDENS

A mere seven miles from Cardiff, lie the splendid Dyffryn Gardens. Within the 50 acres are broad open vistas, distinct garden rooms, a fine arboretum and several glasshouses. Approaching the house, several coniferous mushrooms—created from a green base of Irish yew topped with a cap of golden yew *Taxus baccata* 'Aurea' come into view.

The original Elizabethan manor house was demolished in 1891 when the estate was sold to John Cory and the present house built on the old foundations. To the south of the house, a Victorian garden, complete with formal bedding, was initially laid out. Later, Cory commissioned Thomas Mawson to redesign and extend the garden, but sadly he never lived to see the new design. After his death in 1906, his son, Reginald Cory not only approved Mawson's designs but also contributed in a positive way for he was a keen horticulturalist who financed many plant collectors and went on his own collecting trip to China in 1933. He was therefore eager to grow many plants new to Britain at Dyffryn. Two of the paper-bark maples *Acer griseum* planted in 1911 are from the seed collected by Ernest H Wilson in China.

To compensate for the lack of spectacular views from the house, Mawson created a large open lawn. He writes about this view in his book *The Art and Craft of Garden Making* '. . . the object being to gain a sense of scale, a restful base to the house and a compensating expanse of view from the principal rooms, to make up for the lack of more distant landscape views. To secure variety, we formed a long central canal and lily pond . . .' Beyond the canal, Mawson planned a pavilion overlooking a lake, but he had to abandon this idea when water from the lake flooded cellars in the house.

The canal remains today, and part of Mawson's broad vista is seen in this elevated view from the Magnolia Room which looks out across the croquet lawn. A pair of stone lions guard the entrance to steps leading down to a sundial and the expansive lower lawn with the canal. The centrepiece to the water lily canal is a magnificent bronze Chinese Dragon Bowl, one of several fine oriental bronze statues presented to the Gardens by the Honourable Grenville Morgan in the 1960s. Beyond the canal is an octagonal pool with a central fountain and running along the southern boundary of the lawn is a vine walk with arches covered with ornamental vines. A pair of tiled shelters, known as thunder houses, were added in the 1950s. From the vine walk the south façade can be seen reflected in the open water of the lily canal.

A series of garden rooms were created in a variety of styles by Mawson. Defined by fine yew hedges—one of which is perforated by eleven small apertures looking into the open-air theatre—these rooms include the Roman garden with colonnades and a raised pool in a sunken lawn and the Paved Court complete with a balstraded terrace, dripping fountain and flower beds.

The size of Dyffryn makes it impractical to see everything in a single visit. Inevitably the garden rooms, perennial borders and bedding displays near the house are most popular, but the magnificent trees in the arboretum should not be missed, especially when the deciduous trees have coloured up in the autumn. A large wild flower meadow attracts many native butterflies during the summer—an informal part of a garden full of surprises and delights which deserves greater acclaim.

Water lily canal with Chinese bronze dragon bowl viewed from Magnolia Room. 7 August 1986

A Subterranean Fantasy

GOLDNEY HALL, CLIFTON, BRISTOL

Artificial grottoes succeed best when a plain or rough exterior leads unexpectedly into an ornate cavern. This element of surprise certainly exists at Goldney in Bristol, where an eighteenth-century subterranean grotto is approached via steps leading down to a gothic-arched entrance. On either side of this entrance there is an irregular cave-like opening.

Although several skylights pierce the grotto ceiling, it takes a few moments for eyes to accommodate to the dim interior and so the first sensation is the sound of cascading water. Automatically, this draws you towards a dark, unlit, jagged aperture framing an artificially lit marble statue of Neptune. Reclining in a cave, his right arm supports an urn from which water gushes out cascading down through a narrow rocky passage before the main stream drops directly into a pool, and side streams trickle out through the fluted edge of two pairs of giant clam shells. A dark passage parallel to the cascade leads to another rocky window framing Neptune's profile.

The grotto was the inspiration of Thomas Goldney III, a reputable Bristol banker, who spent considerable time and money embellishing his garden on top of the escarpment overlooking the Avon gorge. Completion of the grotto took twenty-seven years—from 1734 to 1764—but in between times much work was done to the garden above ground, including the construction of the Great Terrace and a rotunda at one end of the Terrace. Built in 1757, the rotunda offered fine views framed by attractive gothick windows with ogee heads, of ships passing along the river Avon. Since then, trees have grown up and blocked the panoramic view.

Goldney kept a Garden Book in which he recorded the constructions and plantings made in the garden. The completion of the shell decorations in the grotto is recorded both in the book 'cover'd and finish'd ye shell of ye Grotto Aug. 1739' and as a shell inscription in the roof of the grotto simply as 17 TG 39. Most of the exotic shells, including giant clams, helmet and cameo shells, originate from tropical Indo-Pacific waters and, since Goldney's father was a shipper and merchant, they were very likely imported directly into Bristol by friends of the family. Other marine shells in the grotto include Mediterranean fan mussels as well as British scallop and necklace shells. Freshwater swan mussels could have come either from Britain or continental Europe.

As well as the shells, there are attractive sea fans (a type of soft coral) branching in a single plane, and clumps of stag's horn coral anchored well above head height just as genuine stag's horn antlers adorn the walls of country mansions and castles. Four huge Tuscan columns supporting the main grotto room are covered with local minerals—so-called Bristol diamonds. No green plants can survive inside the dark interior, but ferns have gained a foothold around the circumference of the ceiling skylights.

Goldney grotto is an excellent example of the way in which a dramatic effect can be achieved, as in the Dinmore Manor grotto (p50), by the juxtaposition of light and shadow. A dark surround automatically arrests attention by forcing the eye to focus beyond the frame on to the lighted area. It also provides a sense of depth to an architectural feature, enhanced by the subtle use of moving water.

A reclining Neptune statue presides at the head of the cascade. 11 December 1983

A Wildlife Haven

In a small country such as Britain, the pressure on land use has resulted in a sharp decline in natural habitats in the last four decades. However, private gardens up and down the country total a million acres, where opportunist wild flowers, insects and birds will move in unaided whenever a suitable niche arises. Chris Baines actively encourages these wildlife invaders into his garden on the outskirts of Birmingham. A landscape architect with a passion for wildlife conservation, he has skilfully designed his third-of-an-acre patch to include a diverse range of habitats specifically aimed at attracting wildlife.

The smallest of gardens can provide a source of water, even if it is only a bird bath, but a pond is more rewarding. Chris Baines has sited his pond well away from overhanging deciduous trees so that few leaves blow in during autumn, but within view of his study window so he can monitor wildlife visitors. It features water-logged areas for marsh-loving plants, a gently sloping side to allow young frogs and toads to crawl out and drops to a depth of at least 2ft/60cm in the centre, so that it never entirely freezes in winter. His remarkably natural-looking pond is fringed by lawn which has been invaded by mosses. The emergent plants include yellow flags *Iris pseudacorus*, greater spearwort *Ranunculus lingua*, lesser reedmace *Typha angustifolia* (less invasive than *T. latifolia*), bogbean *Menyanthes trifoliata* and water mint *Mentha aquatica*. Lesser duckweed *Lemna minor* and fringed waterlily *Nymphoides peltata* pads float on the surface. A plastic duck decoy helps to lure avian visitors; while frogs, toads, newts and dragonflies have also homed in on this pond.

The most colourful part of this view from his study window is his so-called 'cottage garden service station' where a succession of native and exotic herbaceous plants flower, attracting foraging insects. Beyond the pond is a meadow and a woodland edge. An instant wildflower meadow can be achieved by either sowing seed or using pot-grown native plants available from specialist wildflower growers. It can be encouraged simply by raising the cutting edges on a lawnmower by some 1-1½in/3–4cm. Using this technique, only two months after Chris Baines had moved in, lady's smock *Cardamine pratensis* began to flower, enticing orange-tip butterflies to lay their eggs. When this picture was taken, hayrattle *Rhinanthus minor* and ox-eye daisies *Chrysanthemum leucanthemum* were flowering among seeding heads of cowslips *Primula veris* and fritillaries *Fritillaria meleagris*. Chris Baines recommends a meandering path is mown through the meadow, to provide a practical walkway and to show that the meadow has been left uncut intentionally! Privet and laurel hedges have been replaced with native plants—field maple (yellow in autumn), hawthorn (blossom attracts insects and berries provide food for birds and small mammals) and dogrose. The hedge is never cut during the nesting season.

Part of the fun of wildlife gardening is that you never know what may turn up. Since Chris Baines created his garden in 1983, his most exciting visitors have been a woodcock and a muntjac deer. His comment—'within the million acres of private gardens in Britain, if everyone managed just part of their patch for wildlife, the impact on nature conservation would be enormous', is indeed a sobering one.

Chris Baines' wildlife garden includes a pond, meadow and a flower border. 18 June 1987

A Lilliputian World

LAMPORT HALL GARDENS

For more than four centuries, Lamport Hall in Northamptonshire was the home of the Isham family. Sir Edmund Isham planted box around groups of shrubs in 1750 and a century later they had grown into box bowers, only one of which remains today. The underground arches supporting a brick wall no longer exist, but this ingenious design allowed fruit trees to be grown on the southern aspect, while their roots could penetrate the damper soil on the shady, north-facing side. The parkland at Lamport Hall was laid out in the 1820s; but it was the tenth baronet, Sir Charles Isham, who was responsible for the garden's unique feature. Adjacent to the formal Italian garden, also laid out by Sir Charles, was his pride and joy—an almost vertical rock garden complete with crevices and caves simulating an alpine rock face in miniature.

In his handwritten book *Notes on Gnomes and Remarks on Rock Gardens* (1884) Sir Charles records how ever since the rock garden was begun in 1847, it received almost daily improvements. 'There is probably no other piece of ground of such limited dimensions [24ft/7m high 90ft/25m long and 47ft/14m wide] . . . which has received so much minute and constant culture over a period of forty years.' The siting of the rock garden close to the house and facing north, can be explained by Sir Charles' spiritual beliefs which encompassed the fantasy world of fairies and gnomes. Indeed, at the back of his book is an undated photograph showing more than a dozen tiny gnomes decorating the rockery. These gnomes, specially imported from Nuremberg, were the first to be used as ornaments in an English garden; although a garden of miniature figures used to offset miniature fir trees was described and illustrated with woodcuts in J C Loudon's 1850 edition of his *Encyclopedia of Gardening*. Sir Charles' little people, made of terracotta and measuring only 3in/7.5cm high, bore little resemblance to the larger gaudy modern equivalents. The crescent-shaped rock garden was built beneath his bedroom window, so he could keep an ever watchful eye on the gnomes.

Not surprisingly, Sir Charles' delight in a Lilliputian world, coincided with his desire to grow miniature plants; if they were not naturally diminutive, then he cultivated them so their growth remained stunted. He created pygmy spruce firs by removing side branches and partly exposing their roots, so that after more than sixty years, they had grown to only 2–3ft/0.6–0.9m high. Sir Charles also made sure vigorous plants did not swamp other plants or conceal the attractive stonework, so he would not have approved of larger plants added since his time. It was never his intention to produce a rock garden covered in flowers, but in April–May '. . . lavender–coloured 'clouds' and 'waterfalls' of the common aubretia . . .' appeared on the upper rocks and by August, ferns enhanced the stones.

What a dull world it would be without eccentrics such as Sir Charles Isham. When Sir Gyles Isham died in 1976, he bequeathed the estate to the Lamport Hall Trust who intend to restore the unique rockery, complete with gnomes, so that we can once more appreciate Sir Charles' philosophy behind his creation of the rock garden: 'It should exhibit a combination of opposite extremes, the utmost wildness of construction, with the highest cultivation.'

Vertical rock garden viewed from Sir Charles Isham's bedroom. 31 July 1987

A Room With a View

PAÇO DE CALHEIROS

There has been a formal garden on the terrace in front of the Paço de Calheiros, near Ponte de Lima in the Minho region of Portugal, since the early part of the eighteenth century when the existing Manor House was built to replace the original fourteenth-century house. The view is most striking early and late in the day, when the green lines of the low box hedges are accentuated by slanting rays of sun grazing across the top. This view from an upper floor encompasses the garden with its magnificent 'borrowed' vista stretching beyond the orange trees, across the vineyards and terraced fields to the sixteen-arch medieval bridge spanning the river Lima in the far distance.

The neat box edging of the beds, the clipped shrubs and the circular tank are all typical elements of Portuguese gardens which have evolved by utilizing ideas from both eastern and western gardens. Their design incorporates features from Italy and France, notably formal parterres, statuary, and clipped shrubs. The Moorish influence is the water tank, often circular in shape and invariably raised so the elevated water level reflects the sky and trees more effectively than it would in a ground level pool.

Natural terraces are commonplace in Portugal, where there is a tendency to adapt the design of a terraced garden so it fits the natural contours, instead of designing the terrace to the best effect as can be seen in so many elaborate formal French and Italian gardens.

Colour in this garden is used sparingly. As in Japanese gardens in Kyoto, azaleas are clipped into simple shapes so they produce concentrated colour when the massed blooms covering the neat spheres open out.

Other shrubs, including variegated *Euonymus*, are also clipped into simple shapes. Around each spherical azalea a neat band of thrift, *Armeria maritima* has been planted. Before the azaleas bloom, bulbs bring scattered colour to the terrace together with the white and red double daisies, *Bellis perennis* 'Monstrosa', in the bed encircling the fountain. In early summer, roses come into their own. The narrow paths weaving through the box hedges are covered with off-white sand.

Projecting above the front wall, flowering spikes of wisteria can be seen; this climber flourishes in the humid temperate climate of northern Portugal, where it is a popular wall plant. Like vines, it provides welcome shade beneath pergolas or glorietas in the heat of the summer sun. Glorietas are often sited at the end of a pergola, where they provide room to sit out in comfort and view the garden. Camellias also thrive in this part of Portugal. In formal gardens they are clipped into cylinders or spheres, but they also make effective evergreen shelter belts when grown as high hedges, as can be seen in the Institute de Botanica garden in Oporto.

From 1984, the modernized Paço de Calheiros has opened its doors to visitors so they can experience living in a Portuguese family home, sampling the food and wine—including the vinhos verdes—of the Minho region. It was dark when we arrived at the house and so we did not see this impressive view until we folded back the shutters early the following morning. In March, the air was cool, but during the summer heat the sound of water splashing into the tank from the simple fountain nozzle would, no doubt, provide a most welcome cooling effect.

A formal terraced garden in northern Portugal overlooks the Lima Valley. 28 March 1987

FEATURED GARDENS OPEN TO THE PUBLIC

GARDENS featured in this book which are open to the public are listed below. Full addresses and up-to-date times of opening can be found in the following publications which are published annually.

Gardens Open to the Public in England and Wales (National Gardens Scheme) (NGS)

Historic Houses, Castles and Gardens in Great Britain and Ireland (British Leisure Publications)

Scotland's Gardens (Scotland's Gardens Scheme)

Houses, Castles and Gardens (Sheet No 32 Irish Tourist Board)

The National Trust and The National Trust for Scotland each provide their members with listings of properties and gardens.

CHINA

Golden Temple (p126)
Kunming   *daily all year*

Lingering Garden (Liu Yuan) (p124)
Suzhou   *daily all year*

Summer Palace (Yi He Yuan) (p120–121)
Beijing   *daily all year*

Yuantong Temple (p118–119)
Kunming   *daily all year*

ENGLAND

Barnsley House (p44–46)
Barnsley, Cirencester, Gloucestershire
all year Monday–Friday 10–6, first Sundays May, June, July 2–6, other days and parties by appointment

Barrington Court Gardens (p68–69)
Barrington, Ilminster, Somerset
Easter Sunday-end September, Saturday–Wednesday 2–5.30

Bramdean House (p61, 72–74)
Bramdean, Near Alresford, Hampshire
as in NGS book, also by appointment.

Brook Cottage (p106–107)
Alkerton, Banbury, Oxfordshire
1 April–30 October daily by appointment also weekends in NGS book

Broughton Castle (p92–93)
Banbury, Oxfordshire
house and garden 18 May–14 September, Wednesdays and Sundays 2–5 also Thursdays July–August 2–5

Castle Tor (p54–55)
Wellswood, Torquay, Devon
as in NGS book, parties by appointment

Cranborne Manor Gardens (p94–95, 105,140)
Cranborne, Dorset
March–October Wednesdays 9–5

Crossing House, The (p104–105)
Shepreth, Cambridge   *all year, any reasonable time*

Dinmore Manor (p50–51)
near Hereford   *daily all year 10–6*

Elvaston Castle Country Park (p90–91)
near Derby   *all year 9–dusk*

Glendurgan, The National Trust (p20–21, 140)
Mawnan Smith, near Falmouth
March–end October, Mondays, Wednesdays and Fridays (excluding Good Friday) 10.30–5.30

Goldney Hall, University of Bristol (p8, 130–131)
Lower Clifton Hill, Bristol
as in NGS book, other dates on request

Haddon Hall and Gardens (p10, 11 and 66–67)
Bakewell, Derbyshire
April–October Tuesdays–Sundays 11–6 closed Sundays July–August

Hawkstone Park (p33, 76–77)
Weston-under-Redcastle, Shrewsbury
guided tours available on request from Hawkstone Park Hotel

Hestercombe Gardens (p30, 32, 42,61)
Cheddon Fitzpaine, Taunton, Somerset
weekdays all year, some Sundays

Hever Castle and Gardens (p28–29)
near Edenbridge, Kent
daily April–October, gardens 11–6

Iford Manor (p58–60)
near Bradford-on-Avon, Wiltshire
May–July Wednesdays and Sundays 2–5, also Summer Bank Holiday Mondays, groups by appointment

Japanese Garden, The (p116–117)
Cottered, Hertfordshire
by prior arrangement

Kew Gardens See Royal Botanic Gardens, Kew

Lamport Hall Gardens (p134–135)
Lamport Hall Trust, Lamport, Northampton
daily Easter-end September 2.15–5.15, other times by prior arrangement

Lanhydrock, The National Trust (p96–97)
near Bodmin, Cornwall
daily 1 April–31 October 11–6, November–March daylight hours

Leeds, 30 Latchmere Road (p112–114)
July–August, Sundays 2.30–6

Lindisfarne Castle, The National Trust (p24–25)
Holy Island, Northumberland
April–September, daily (closed Friday) 11–5. October Saturday and Sunday 11–5. Garden opened by contacting the Administrator (0289) 89244

London, 29 Deodar Road (p102–103)
Putney
as in NGS book

The Manor House, Chenies (p61, 108–109)
Rickmansworth, Hertfordshire
April–October Wednesdays and Thursdays 2–5

Moseley Old Hall, The National Trust (p36–37)
Fordhouses, Wolverhampton
12 March–26 June, (not Good Friday) 17 September–30 October Saturdays and Sundays 2–6. 29 June–11 September Wednesdays–Sundays 2–6

Painshill Park (p33, 38–39)
Painshill Park Trust Ltd, Sandown House, High Street, Esher, Surrey
as the garden is still being restored, the Park is not fully open to visitors, please ring (0932) 68113 for details

Parnham House (front cover, p15, 48, 49, 140)
Beaminster, Dorset
Sundays, Wednesdays and Bank Holidays 10–5, group visits by arrangement

Penshurst Place (back cover, p86, 88)
Tunbridge Wells, Kent
daily, except Monday, 1 April–first Sunday in October 12.30–6, open Bank Holiday Mondays

Rodmarton Manor (p78–79)
near Cirencester, Gloucestershire
as in NGS book and every Wednesday afternoon March–August

Royal Botanic Gardens, Kew (p22–23)
Kew, Richmond, Surrey
daily all year 9.30–dusk, closed Christmas Day and New Year's Day

Stone House Cottage Gardens (p52–53)
Stone (on A448), near Kidderminster, Worcestershire
April–October Wednesdays–Saturdays 10–6 also Sundays May–June

Sudeley Castle (p82–83)
Winchcombe, Gloucestershire   *daily April–October 11–5.30*

Sutton Park (p26–27, 61)
Sutton-on-the-Forest, North Yorkshire
April–October 11.30–5.30

Tudor Garden, The (p34–35)
Tudor House Museum, Bugle Street, Southampton
all year Tuesday–Saturday 10–5, Sunday 2–5, closed Monday, Christmas Day and Boxing Day

IRELAND
Heywood Garden at Salesian College (p75, 84–85)
Ballinakill, Portlaoise   *open to those interested by appointment*

Japanese Gardens (p122–123)
Tully, Kildare, County Kildare
daily Easter–end October, weekdays 10–5, Saturdays and public holidays 10–5.30, Sundays 2–5.30

National Botanic Gardens (p40–41)
Glasnevin, Dublin
daily, excluding Christmas Day, 1 March–end October, weekdays 9–6, Sundays 11–6, 1 November–end February weekdays 10–4.30, Sundays 11–4.30

PORTUGAL
Paço de Calheiros (p136–137)
Calheiros 4990, Ponte de Lima, Portugal   *daily all year*

SCOTLAND
Crathes Castle, The National Trust for Scotland (p64–65, 79)
Banchory, Grampian Region
daily all year 9.30–sunset

Drummond Castle (p98–100)
Muthill, Tayside Region
daily May–August inc., 2–6, last entry 5, September Wednesday and Sunday only

USA
GEORGIA
Savannah private garden (p70–71)
by appointment with Historic Savannah Foundation

WALES
Dyffryn Gardens (p128–129)
St Nicholas, Cardiff
daily all year, admission charged end March–end October

PHOTOGRAPHIC NOTES

ONE of the first permanent photographs ever taken was a view from a casement window in Le Gras by Nicephore Niépce in 1827. The exposure for his heliograph, or sun picture, was thought to have taken eight hours, during which time the movement of the sun from east to west completely destroyed the modelling we can now achieve using short exposures in direct sunlight. In recent years, the production of very fast films with speeds of 1600–3200 ISO, enables photographs to be taken in any situation during the day or night. Such films will not produce the high definition required for book reproduction and so slow speed films were used here.

Many garden photographers maintain that the only time to record gardens in temperate regions during the summer is either early in the morning between the hours of 4.30–8.00 am or late in the evening between 6–9 pm. However, since there are so many variable factors affecting the direction and quality of light, I am prepared to be more flexible. From dawn to dusk, the angle and intensity of the light are constantly changing. The angle of the sun also depends on the latitude and the season. Together with landscape photographers, I prefer to avoid working when the sun is high in the sky, because the shadows are short and hence the modelling poor, although the steep-sided south-facing valley at Glendurgan (p21) had to be taken late in the morning to avoid excessive cross shadows. On flatter sites, a low-angled sun will provide a greater three-dimensional feeling to a two-dimensional photograph. Early morning light is often magical; but gaining access to a house before people are normally awake is difficult— unless the best view happens to be from the guest bedroom.

At the beginning and end of the day, the low-angled lighting casts large areas of strong shadow. While these can add interest to a large lawn, such as at Parnham (p49) it is often extremely difficult to bring out details when the shadow falls across a border. The colour temperature also changes early and late in the day, because some of the blue light is absorbed as the low-angled sun passes through a thicker layer of the atmosphere, thereby giving the picture a reddish cast. On completely overcast days, a bluish cast may appear in pictures of green plants and snow-covered ground, because some red light is absorbed by the clouds. Any garden or nature photographer who aims to reproduce authentic greens on colour film, will find a warming filter invaluable for correcting the otherwise cold colours recorded on overcast days. These filters are amber-coloured, and either the 81B or the slightly warmer 81C will help to warm natural greens. On very bright days, a polarizing filter can be used to enrich all colours by removing highlights and skylight reflections from shiny leaves and fruit or smooth water surfaces.

Gardens are rarely open to, or seen by, visitors early or late in the day; so only a few photographs for this book were taken then. The photography was done at varying times, depending on the aspect, the time of year and the nature of the available light. Since the position of the window determined the camera viewpoint, an initial reconnaissance usually had to be made to assess the best time of day for photography. Consequently, most gardens had to be visited at least twice and, in some cases, owing to the vagaries of the British weather, three times. When gardens enclosed by high walls—such as the Spanish courtyard garden on page 17—are lit by bright sunlight, they invariably have a strong shadow across them; so they are best photographed in the soft diffuse light of an overcast day. This type of lighting also works well for muted colour pictures as seen in the spring view of Cranborne Manor knot garden (page 95).

The original aim for illustrating this book was to frame all the views with the window. However, as anyone who has looked through a small window will know, the angle of view can be quite limiting and it may not offer the best vista of a garden. A wider angle of view can be gained by moving closer to the window, but even if an ultra-wide angle lens is used, it can still be a problem getting both the frame and the vista sharply in focus. For this reason, it was decided that wherever the frame limited the scope of the view, the picture would have to be taken through an open window. When a view had to be photographed through glass, the problems encountered were similar to aquarium photography. Firstly, the glass needed to be as clean as possible and blemish-free otherwise the view would have been distorted. Secondly, care had to be taken to avoid getting reflections of my hands and the camera in the glass, so I then worked behind a black velvet screen with a central hole for the camera lens.

The majority of the photographs were taken on Hasselblad cameras with lenses ranging from 38mm–250mm on Professional Ektachrome 64 film. On overcast days, I substituted Nikons and used Kodachrome 25 film, which gives better colour reproduction under these conditions. When working in confined spaces, perspective distortion can result from diverging foregrounds and converging verticals. To overcome this problem, a 28mm perspective-correcting Nikon lens was used for some architectural features. The versatile Benbo tripod allowed me to work in some bizarre situations including inside an ancient bath tub and on the boulder strewn floor of a grotto.

From experience of working at sub-zero temperatures in Britain, special precautions were taken to ensure the camera batteries would not fail when working at −20°C at Harbin in China. The Nikon F3 was powered by a special cold weather battery pack kept warm inside my anorak. In this way, I was able to use the camera on a tripod for several hours at a stretch taking many $\frac{1}{2}$- and 1-second exposure pictures of the illuminated ice sculptures at night (p118).

ACKNOWLEDGEMENTS

I SHOULD like to thank everybody who so willingly gave their time to answer my queries. In particular, the Royal Horticultural Society's staff at Wisley Garden and at the Lindley Library, and the British Architectural Library. Additional help was forthcoming from The British Library, The Glass Manufacturers Association, The Museum of London, the National Gallery, The National Trust, The National Trust for Scotland, Pilkington Glass Ltd Communications Service, the Society of Landscape Designers, the School of Oriental and African Studies at the University of London, the Victoria and Albert Museum, several county organizers for The National Gardens Scheme and several members of The Garden History Society.

Many individuals were also a tremendous help in suggesting gardens or supplying information, in particular:
William E Alexander Landscape Manager Biltmore Estate,
Mavis Batey, William L Beiswanger, Richard Bisgrove, Nicola Gordon Bowe, Patrick Bowe, Catherine Choiseul, Brian Coe Curator The National Centre of Photography, Gina and Peter Corrigan of Occidor Limited, Nicholas Day, C Douglas Deane, Ruth Duthie, Paul Edwards, Robert Gimson, Jack Jones, Mary Keeling of The Colonial Williamsburg Foundation, Dr Bill Klein, Dr Sylvia Landsberg, Alicia Moguilevsky, Elizabeth McLean, Lord Neidpath, Dr E Charles Nelson, Rita Skinner, Dr Christopher Thacker, Dr Michael Tooley, Rosemary Verey, Elena Villa, Paul Walsh, Louisa Farrand Wood, Tom Woodhams

I am indebted to the following publishers and authors for permission to quote copyright material from their books:
On pages 13 and 101
From *Mediaeval Gardens* by John Harvey published by B. T. Batsford Ltd, London and quoted with the publisher's permission.
On pages 16, 19 and 80
From *The Education of a Gardener* by Russell Page, published by Collins Ltd.
On page 100
From *Stately Gardens of Britain* © Thomas Hinde 1983, produced by Tigerlily Ltd and published by Ebury Press.
On page 16
From *Garden Design* by David Hicks published by Routledge & Kegan Paul (Associated Book Publishers UK Ltd)

I would especially like to thank my mother, Hazel Le Rougetel, for her help throughout the project; Colour Processing Laboratories for their efficient film processing service; Jane Mulleneux and Renée van der Most for assisting in the research who, together with Rona Tiller, transferred my handwritten script onto a word processor. Finally, I am as always, indebted to my husband, Martin Angel, for his constant help and encouragement.

In addition, I am most grateful to the following who so kindly allowed me to photograph from their windows and also the gardeners whose devoted work has maintained the views. My thanks are also extended to many other owners who very kindly gave me access, with apologies for being unable to include their garden. This was because my specific brief and restrictive viewpoints, did not do justice to their garden; rather than to any deficiencies in the garden itself.

The Irish National Stud, The National Trust, The National Trust for Scotland, The Trustees of the Grimsthorpe and Drummond Castle Trust Ltd and Lady Willoughby de Eresby, James and Louisa Arbuthnott, The Lady Ashcombe, Marigold Assinder, Professor Chris Baines, Mrs Anthony Biddulph, Joe and Frieda Brown, Mario de Rosirio Calheiros, Viscount de L'Isle VC, KG, Derbyshire County Council Planning Department, Dyffryn House Conference Centre and Gardens, Mr and Mrs Guy Elmes, Margaret and Douglas Fuller, Douglas and Susan Hamilton, Hawkstone Park Hotels Ltd, Hever Castle Ltd, John and Elizabeth Hignett, Mr and Mrs David Hodges, The Lamport Hall Trust, Mr Andrew Lyle, Ann McPhail, Jennie and John Makepeace, Lt Col and Mrs Macleod Matthews, James Morton, Mr R G Murray, National Botanic Gardens Glasnevin Dublin, The Painshill Park Trust, Royal Botanic Gardens Kew, His Grace the Duke of Rutland CBE, Salesian College, The Marchioness of Salisbury, The Lord and Lady Sele, Mrs Nancie Sheffield, The Duquesa de Soma, The Somerset Fire Brigade, Southampton City Council, Leonard Stocks, The University of Bristol and The Warden of Goldney House, Rosemary Verey, Mrs Hady Wakefield, Mr and Mrs John Wallinger, Susan and Graeme Woodhatch

BIBLIOGRAPHY

ALL of these sources have been consulted at first hand during research for *A View From A Window*. Ray Desmond's *Bibliography of British Gardens*, St Paul's Bibliographies, Winchester, 1984 was an invaluable initial source for references, particularly for historical accounts of gardens.

The six volumes in *The Gardens of Britain* series published by Batsford, London, 1977–1979 were also referred to repeatedly.

Vol 1 *Devon and Cornwall* by Patrick M Synge
Vol 2 *Dorset, Hampshire and the Isle of Wight* by Allen Paterson
Vol 3 *Berkshire, Oxfordshire, Buckinghamshire, Bedfordshire and Hertfordshire* by Richard Bisgrove
Vol 4 *Kent, East and West Sussex and Surrey* by Tom Wright
Vol 5 *Yorkshire and Humberside* by Ken Lemmon
Vol 6 *Derbyshire, Leicestershire, Lincolnshire, Northamptonshire and Nottinghamshire* by John Anthony

Angel, Heather *A Camera in the Garden*, Quiller Press, London, 1984

Baines, Chris *How to Make a Wildlife Garden*, Elm Tree Books, London, 1985

Beck, Thomasina *Embroidered Gardens*, Angus & Robertson Ltd., London, 1979.

Blomfield, Reginald *The Formal Garden in England*, Macmillan, London, 1892

Bord, Janet *Mazes and Labyrinths of the World*, Latimer New Dimensions, London, 1976

Brent, Elliott *Victorian Gardens*, Batsford, London, 1986

Brookes, John *The Small Garden*, Marshall Cavendish Books, London, 1977

Clery, Val *Windows: A feast for the eye and the imagination*, Penguin Books, Harmondsworth, 1978

Coate, Randoll, Adrian Fisher & Graham Burgess *A Celebration of Mazes*, Minotaur Designs, St Albans, 1986

Coats, Peter *Great Gardens of Britain*, Hamlyn, Feltham, 1970

Cook, F Palmer *Talk to me of Windows*, Witt Allen, London & New York, 1971

Fleming, Laurence & Alan Gore *The English Garden*, Michael Joseph, London, 1979

Forsyth, Alastair *Yesterday's Gardens*, HMSO, London, 1983

Glass Manufacturers Federation *Making Glass*, 1985

Grigson, Geoffrey *The Englishman's Flora*, Phoenix House, London, 1958

Hadfield, Miles *A History of British Gardening*, Hamlyn, Feltham, 1969 (rev. edn.)

Harris, John *A Garden Alphabet*, Octopus Books Ltd., London, 1979.

Harvey, John *Mediaeval Gardens*, Batsford, London, 1981

Hellyer, Arthur *Gardens of Genius*, Hamlyn, Feltham, 1980

Hicks, David *Garden Design*, Routledge & Kegan Paul, London, 1982

Inn, Henry & Shao Chang Lee *Chinese Houses and Gardens*, Hastings House, New York, 1940

Jacques, David *Georgian Gardens: The Reign of Nature*, Batsford, London, 1983

Jekyll, Gertrude *Wall and Water Gardens*, Country Life, London, 1901

Jekyll, Gertrude *Colour Schemes for the Flower Garden*, Country Life, London, 1908

Jellicoe, George & Susan *The Landscape of Man*, Thames & Hudson, London, 1987 (rev. edn.)

Jellicoe, George & Susan, Patrick Goode & Michael Lancaster (eds.) *The Oxford Companion to Gardens*, Oxford University Press, Oxford, 1986

Jones, Barbara *Follies and Grottoes*, Constable, London, 1974 (2nd edn.)

Kuck, Loraine *The World of the Japanese Garden*, John Weatherhill, New York & Tokyo, 1968

Lees-Milne, Alvilde & Rosemary Verey (eds.) *The Englishwoman's Garden*, Penguin Books, London, 1980

Lees-Milne, Alvilde & Rosemary Verey (eds.) *The Englishman's Garden*, Penguin Books, London, 1982

Lloyd, Nathaniel *A History of the English House*, Omega Books, Ware, 1985

Malins, Edward & Patrick Bowe *Irish Gardens and Demesnes from 1830*, Barrie & Jenkins, London, 1980

Oliver, Paul *Dwellings: The House across the World*, Phaidon, Oxford, 1987

Page, Russell *The Education of a Gardener*, Collins, London, 1983

Patrick, John *The Australian Garden*, Nelson, Victoria, 1985

Siren, Osvald *Gardens of China*, Ronald Press, New York, 1949

Strong, Roy *The Renaissance Garden in England*, Thames & Hudson, London, 1979

Tait, A A *The Landscape Garden in Scotland 1735–1835*, Edinburgh University Press, 1980

Thacker, Christopher *The History of Gardens*, Croom Helm, London, 1979

Thomas, Graham Stuart *Gardens of the National Trust*, The National Trust/Weidenfeld and Nicolson, London, 1979

Triggs, H Inigo *Formal gardens in England and Scotland*, Batsford, London, 1902

Verey, Rosemary & Ellen Samuels *The American Woman's Garden*, Little, Brown & Company, Boston, 1984

Villiers-Stuart, C M *Spanish Gardens* Batsford, London, 1929

INDEX

Featured gardens are listed on pp 138–9; **Bold** numbers are plates